Educating Immigrant Students

What We Need to Know to Meet the Challenges

Xue Lan Rong
Judith Preissle

CORWIN PRESS, INC.
A Sage Publications Company
Thousand Oaks, California

For information:

Corwin Press, Inc.
A Sage Publications Company
2455 Teller Road
Thousand Oaks, California 91320
E-mail: order@corwin.sagepub.com

SAGE Publications Ltd.
6 Bonhill Street
London EC2A 4PU
United Kingdom

SAGE Publications India Pvt. Ltd.
M-32 Market
Greater Kailash I
New Delhi 110 048 India

Printed in the United States of America

Library of Congress Cataloging-in-Publication Data

Rong, Xue Lan.
  Educating immigrant children : what we need to know to meet the challenges / by Xue Lan Rong, Judith Preissle.
    p. cm.
  Includes bibliographical references and index.
  ISBN 0-8039-6306-8 (pbk.: acid-free paper). — ISBN 0-8039-6305-X (cloth: acid-free paper)
    1. Immigrants—Education—United States. 2. Children of immigrants—Education—United States. 3. Educational anthropology—United States. 4. Educational sociology—United States.
  I. Preissle, Judith. II. Title.
  LC3731.X84 1997
  371.826'91—dc21   97-21202

This book is printed on acid-free paper.

98 99 00 01 02 03 10 9 8 7 6 5 4 3 2 1

Production Editor: Sherrise M. Purdum
Production Assistant: Karen Wiley
Typesetter/Designer: Danielle Dillahunt
Indexer: Teri Greenberg
Cover Designer: Marcia M. Rosenburg
Print Buyer: Anna Chin

Contents

Acknowledgments

Two grants awarded Xue Lan Rong benefited our research—a 1995 Junior Faculty Development Award and a 1996-1997 grant from the Institute for Research in Social Science of the University of North Carolina at Chapel Hill. Xuguang Guo's assistance in assembling census data and Elizabeth Koehler's editorial aid have been invaluable. We have depended on the attention and support of our partners, Cong Yuan and Mark Toomey, and of our loving siblings—Bing and Alice, Pete and Rob. The late Professor Everett Keach provided us many years of help and encouragement. Finally, Professor Frank Brown of the University of North Carolina helped us talk each other into exploring what census data mean for all of us.

XUE LAN RONG
Chapel Hill, North Carolina

JUDITH PREISSLE
Athens, Georgia

About the Authors

Xue Lan Rong, Assistant Professor at the University of North Carolina, Chapel Hill, is a first-generation immigrant whose native language is Chinese. As a classroom teacher and teacher educator, she has more than 15 years of teaching experience in public schools at various levels in the United States and China. Her expertise in immigration-related educational issues comes through two kinds of experiences. Her first-hand experience is based on a long-time working relationship with immigrant children, their parents, and their ethnic communities. This book is a reflection of her own experience as an immigrant teacher in and out of the classroom, as a consulting expert in developing curriculum and programs, and as an immigrant researcher, in dialogue with the academic community. She obtained her research experience via sociological, demographic, and pedagogical training. She has continually published in major sociological and educational journals and presented at national conferences on the topics of generation, race and ethnicity, national origins, gender, social class, and educational attainment and achievement of immigrant children since 1988, when she finished her dissertation at the University of Georgia.

Judith Preissle, Professor at the University of Georgia, is a graduate of Indiana University—a teacher educator and an educational anthropologist who brings a dual insider-outsider perspective to issues of education and immigration. She is a native-born citizen of the United

States whose forebears arrived on the continent in the 18th and 19th centuries. She is also one of the many internal migrants of the 20th century, who grew up moving around the country and attending schools in six different states. Beginning her educational experience teaching social studies and language arts to 12-year-olds, she has spent the past 23 years at the University of Georgia teaching the social foundations of education, qualitative research methods, and educational anthropology to an increasingly diverse population of graduates and undergraduates. She has published widely in these areas with special concentration on sociocultural theory and on gender and minority education.

Introduction

What makes educating immigrant children today different from the early 20th century when the nation and its schools faced another peak of immigration? Today's educators face three new challenges. First, the non-European background of the majority of immigrants makes traditional education in English and conventional assimilation practices exceedingly difficult. Second, the debates on multiculturalism and pluralism in both schools and the broader society make educating immigrant children increasingly complex. Third, recent immigrants are very diverse in national origin, culture, socioeconomic background, and legal status. This diversity demands a wide variety of services—linguistic, curricular, and instructional—from underprepared teachers and ill-equipped urban schools, already overstressed with diminishing resources. To work well with immigrant children, educators must understand immigrant, cultural, and ethnic diversity in communities in the United States, examine and clarify their own racial and ethnic attitudes, and develop appropriate pedagogical knowledge and skills.

In this book we address these concerns, considering the shortcomings and assets of existing knowledge and the implications for educating immigrant populations traditionally underserved in U.S. public schools. Since the 1970s, when the current wave of immigration began, many scholars have studied particular groups of immigrants, but no national profile has been published of the educational status of immigrant children. Our book addresses the need for a nationwide, current view of what is happening to immigrants in schools today. A second issue on information about immigrants is that, until recently, survey data grouped people only in the broadest categories—Asian, for example—with no finer distinction by nation or even region of origin. Our profile distinguishes immigrants not only by region and nation of origin, but also by three generations—newcomers, newcomers' children born in the United States, and grandchildren of immigrants. The focus is, however, the first generation, immigrant children and adolescents aged 5-18.

Our assessment of the current immigration situation and of the characteristics of new immigrants provides educational policymakers and administrators at various levels with the information needed to project school enrollment and staff recruitment and development as well as curriculum and program construction. Knowledge of immigration, immigrants, and the history of U.S. immigration and immigrants' schooling provides the nation's educators with understanding, insight, and perspective on the new immigration movement and on how our society and schools can adapt effectively to the changes.

We intend this book to be a scholarly work accessible to the educated public. Based on the sketch we draw from 1990 census data and demographers' population projections, we make recommendations for educational policymakers, school administrators, and classroom teachers who are working in areas where the immigrant population is and will be rapidly growing. We hope that teacher educators and other educational faculty of colleges and universities also will find this profile of immigrants and their education to be useful in courses in educational leadership, multicultural education, and the social foundations of education.

Content of the Book

In this book we focus on the education of immigrant students. Ten chapters examine immigration and how it interacts with race, ethnicity, nationality, gender, social class, and residential location as these are addressed by theories and practices of schooling. Three interrelated approaches guide us: We explore the current information on immigrants and their schooling; we examine how racial and ethnic socialization of immigrant minority children is conceptualized; by suggesting how the educational experiences of immigrant students may differ among themselves and from those of other students, we seek to create a forum for dialogue on this topic that reaches local, regional, national, and international levels.

The first four chapters are an overview of factors and issues in immigration and education in the United States and a summary of the most current information on the socioeconomic, demographic, linguistic, and educational characteristics of U.S. immigrant children and adolescents aged 5-18. Chapter 1, Immigration and Schooling in the United States, is an overview of who current immigrants are, how they compare to previous immigrants, and what the immigrant experience in schools has been. Chapter 2, Families and Communities, examines current immigrants—adults and children—in more detail for how they are different from one another and for where they settle in their new country. Chapter 3, Overcoming Language Barriers, focuses on the status of immigrant children's language proficiency—English acquisition and the retention or attrition of native languages. Chapter 4, Educational Attainment, compares the educational achievement of immigrants and their native-born children and grandchildren with that of other students.

The next two chapters examine the racial and ethnic identity reconstruction of immigrant minority children and its implication for their schooling. Chapter 5, Learning New Cultures, presents theories and beliefs about the relationship between immigrants and their new societies, focusing especially on the transformation of immigrant minority children's identities—racial, ethnic, and other—in their encounter with the new society. Chapter 6, Learning in School, uses a comprehensive cultural-contextual interactive approach to identify and differentiate the causes of variations in educational performance and its related problems among different groups of immigrant children.

The following three chapters describe the different groups of people dominating current immigration, discussing groups by areas of geographic origin: Latin America, Asia, and Africa and the Caribbean. Chapter 7, Hispanic Children; Chapter 8, Asian Children; and Chapter 9, Caribbean and African Black Children, place multiculturalism and pluralism in a broad historical, comparative, and international context. Each chapter uses a similar format to examine an issue: We present the issue as it is currently formulated; we analyze the issue with census data and field theories; we summarize the chapter, draw conclusions, and make recommendations.

Chapter 10, The Future for Immigrant Children, ends our discussion with a brief review and summary. We draw on the material we have synthesized to identify ongoing problems and issues and to make recommendations and consider implications for policy and practice.

Knowledge Base

We use two sources of knowledge for this book: empirical research studies and conceptual material from the literature. The empirical studies comprise two categories: primary data we have analyzed and secondary data we cite from other researchers' studies. Primary data are quantitative aggregated data or individual data on magnetic tapes or CD-ROM from U.S. government agencies, mainly the U.S. Bureau of the Census and the National Center for Educational Statistics (see Sources of Information, pp. 153-155). Secondary data are material cited from empirical research conducted by others: quantitative studies conducted by demographers, sociologists, and social psychologists and qualitative studies conducted by anthropologists, other ethnographers, psychologists, and educational researchers. The conceptual material from the literature includes theoretical frameworks, policy formulations and other position statements, and anecdotal accounts from participants. These come from the philosophy and psychology of education, critical sociology, cultural anthropology, multicultural theory, and literary criticism. From time to time, we also draw from our own lives, experiences, education, and teaching.

In characterizing people and groups, we have used the terms offered in the 1990 census by which individuals classified themselves. These classifications are hotly debated labels, of course, but nevertheless do represent a nationwide image. Researchers report great variation within each supernationality group, Hispanic, Asian, and black immigrants (Portes & Rumbaut, 1996). We work with such a large census database that we can examine adequate information on immigrant children for each subgroup. Our initial data analysis used a total of 109,000 immigrant youth. We group immigrant children at three levels for comparison and contrast:

1. Race or supernationality: Asian, Hispanic, black, and white;
2. Ethnicity or subsupernationality: non-Hispanic whites from English language countries, non-Hispanic whites from non-English

language countries, Caribbean blacks, African blacks, Mexicans, Hispanics other than Mexican, Asians other than Southeast Asians, Southeast Asians;

3. Region or nationality: Haitians, Jamaicans, Africans, Mexicans, Dominicans, Cubans, Central Americans, South Americans, Chinese, Japanese, Koreans, Asian Indians, Filipinos, Southeast Asians.

In addition to these groupings, we consider what are called cohorts of immigrants and their children. Cohorts are those who arrived in the United States during the same time period. For comparison our focus is these cohorts: 1975-1979, 1980-1981, 1982-1984, 1985-1986, and 1987-1990.

1

Immigration and Schooling in the United States

Although all countries have experienced immigration, no country in the world has constantly experienced such a high immigration rate over such a long time period as the United States. The international migration rate is so high that almost everyone, except Native Americans, in the United States today is either an immigrant or the descendant of 60 million immigrants. The census of 1990 showed that 20% of the U.S. population was either a first- or second-generation immigrant and that 87% identified themselves by either single or multiple migrant ancestry. In the 1980s, immigration contributed a third of the population growth in the nation.

Immigration is integral to the American society that began to develop with the influx of European and African peoples in the 16th century. Immigration to this country, however, has varied considerably over the centuries, both in magnitude and composition. Between 1820, when statistics on immigration first became available, and 1990, about 60 million immigrants entered the country. During 6 of the 11 years from 1905 through 1915, more than a million immigrants arrived each year. In 1907, the peak year, the number of immigrants reached 1.3 million, and there were several years when 750,000 or more entered the

2

United States. The annual number fluctuated with prosperity and depression, war and peace, and at its lowest point in this century, 1934, only 20,000 immigrants entered. The current wave of immigrants since 1980 has been the largest since the 1910s, which saw one of the twin peaks of immigration in the 20th century and brought more than 1,000 immigrant children per day to settle in the United States and enter its schools.

The recent immigrants are also the most diversified people in race, ethnicity, and socioeconomic status. As a result of the newest wave of immigrants, American society and schools face several demographically based challenges in the years ahead and must change fundamentally to cope with them.

According to population projections (Edmonston & Passel, 1992), U.S. total population is expected to grow steadily from 252 million in 1990 to 350 million in the next 50 years, with a fairly large share of non-white population. The growth rates for the white non-Hispanic population are 12% per decade, or less than 1.2% per year between 1900 to 1990, and the black population has grown steadily from 9 million in 1900 to 30 million in 1990. In contrast, the Hispanic population has grown rapidly—from less than 1 million at the turn of the century to 22 million in 1990. This fast growth represents a compounded growth rate of 48% per decade, or 4% per year for 90 years. The Asian population in the United States has shown a similar pattern of rapid growth—from less than 250,000 in 1900 to 7.3 million in 1990, an average annual increase of 3.8%. These figures indicate not only a trend toward a growing proportion of minorities in the total population, but also one of the most dramatic effects of immigration—a significant shift occurring within the minority population itself. The proportion of the minority population consisting of blacks has been decreasing steadily. For the first time in U.S. history, blacks will account for less than one half of the minority population. This shift has profound implications for political and social relationships between whites and blacks and among racial and ethnic groups in the United States.

In this chapter we address these basic questions: Who are these newcomers, when do they come, where do they come to, how do they come, and why do they come? How do Americans receive them, then and now? We address these questions by exploring the current wave of immigration to the United States in the context of the past century and the future, from 1900 to 2050, with a focus on the next 25 years. Using U.S. census data and other demographic data, we first describe the new immigrants' numbers and origins, their demographic characteristics, and what their impact has been and will be on the composition of the U.S. population, generational and racial. The social and schooling history of immigrants, focusing on the 5- to 18-year-old age group, also is reviewed.

The New Immigration Movement and the New Immigrants

The United States has undergone substantial demographic changes in the past half century as a result of post-1965 immigration. These changes are reflected in the data published by U.S. government agencies and in the research literature. The diversification and transformation of U.S. society induced by this new immigration are well established.

According to demographers (e.g., Martin & Midgley, 1994), American ancestry can be categorized three ways:

1. *Colonists:* European colonists laid the framework of the society that later became the United States in the early 17th century at Jamestown and Plymouth.
2. *Involuntary Americans:* Two kinds of coercion were used to incorporate people into U.S. society: the shipment of African slaves whose descendants composed 19% of the U.S. population in 1890—an estimated 600,000 involuntary African immigrants had been brought by the slave trade before the 1808 abolition of the importation of slaves; and the incorporation of Native American, Spanish, and French populations as the boundaries of the United States expanded westward.
3. *Immigrants:* Here we define *immigrant* to mean an alien who has voluntarily moved from one society to another. Some 60 million immigrants have come to the United States since its founding. They, along with colonists, slaves, Native Americans, and their descendants, make up the American people; by the end of the 20th century, of course, many Americans claim ancestry from more than one of these groups.

Noncitizens enter the United States legally in three ways: immigrants whose numbers are limited by the quota; refugees or others seeking asylum whose numbers are not always restricted to the quota (this is also called "additional immigration"); and nonimmigrants, such as visitors for various long-term or short-term purposes. Using 1994 as an example, 15% of immigrants were professionals, and another 15% were refugees or asylees. The large majority (almost 60%) of immigrants were relatives of U.S. citizens or of permanent residents. "Additional immigration" made up the remaining 12% of newcomers entering the United States in 1994 under special programs or categories (Martin & Midgley, 1994).

Those who enter the United States or who postpone their departure without Immigration and Naturalization Service (INS) permission are called illegal aliens, a government term, or undocumented immigrants, an academic term. By a conservative estimate, the number of undocumented immigrants living in the United States in the mid-1990s ranges from 3 million to 6 million people. About 300,000 people have been entering every year since the 1970s (Martin & Midgley, 1994; Passel & Woodrow, 1984). Roughly half of those who have no U.S. visas crossed the border without being apprehended. The remainder entered the country legally but violated their visa limits.

The United States is in the midst of a wave of immigration with no sign that it will slow down. Immigration is and will be one of the most critical demographic factors in this country for the next 50 years. Immigration to the United States in the past several years has reached the same levels as the period of peak immigration in 1910—nearly one million arrivals per year since the late 1970s including both legal and undocumented immigrants. Approximately half of the total U.S. foreign-born population arrived in America between 1980 and 1990.

Changes in General Characteristics

The new immigration is different in many aspects from U.S. immigration patterns of the past. First, the new pattern has a larger proportion of "additional immigration" than any cohort in U.S. history. This additional immigration is comprised mainly of refugees and undocumented immigrants, but it also includes asylees, amnestied immigrants, and various categories not included as "immigrants" by the INS. Over a million Cubans have been the largest group of refugees to be admitted to the United States since the end of World War II. About 850,000 persons from southeast Asian nations make up the second largest group of refugees to have been admitted. During the 10-year period from 1975 to 1986, other large groups of refugees entered the country:

for example, 109,000 Soviet refugees, 30,000 Poles, 26,000 Rumanians, 21,000 Afghans, 18,000 Ethiopians, and 6,000 Iraqis. With this additional immigration, 1981-1990 may be the decade with the largest amount of immigration in the history of the United States, surpassing the 1901-1910 decade (Martin & Midgley, 1994).

Second, although many of the newcomers to the United States can qualify as the "huddled masses" named on the Statue of Liberty, a larger proportion of the new immigrants are the educated, the skilled, and even the affluent and powerful of other nations. This is evident in the current immigrants' educational attainments. Although the least educated of today's immigrants are only half as likely as native-born Americans to have finished high school, the most educated immigrants are more likely than the native born to have graduate and professional degrees.

Third, immigration has changed and will continue to alter the ethnic composition of the American population. Of immigrants arriving today, 9 of 10 are from non-European countries. Asian and Latin American countries, together, sent 85% of all U.S. immigrants during the 1980s; Mexico, the Philippines, China, Korea, and Vietnam were the top five countries of origin sending the most immigrants to the United States during the 1980s.

Within race and ethnic groups, nationality variations can be dramatic (cf., e.g., Kong & Preissle, 1994; Rumbaut, 1994). Rumbaut has argued that today's immigrants include the most-educated groups (e.g., Asian Indians and Taiwanese) and the least-educated groups (e.g., Mexicans and Salvadorans) as well as groups with the lowest poverty rates (Filipinos) and the highest poverty rates (Laotians and Cambodians)—a reflection of polarized migrant backgrounds from vastly different historical and structural contexts. He has suggested that today's immigrants also differ greatly in their English language skills, age and sex patterns, and family size and organization.

In summary, by any description, this is a new immigration pattern, a phenomenon to be accommodated effectively and conscientiously by educators in the United States.

Changes in Generational Composition

As immigrants flow into the country, they affect the composition of the population in several ways that result in changes across different generations of Americans (Edmonston & Passel, 1992).

First, they increase the foreign-born population in absolute numbers and in the proportion of immigrants and native-born children of immigrant parents in the population. The foreign-born population, 22.4 million, is now the highest in the United States since the previous peak of immigration in 1910. The population of native-born children of immigrants is also at an all-time high since 1910: 25 million. In 1990, about 47 million persons were either foreign-born or had at least one foreign-born parent, a number accounting for almost 22% of the population. If this turnaround in growth that started in the 1960s continues, a quarter of the U.S. population in 25 years (2023) will be immigrants and their children.

This large contribution of immigration to population growth has occurred before. As much as two fifths of the population increase during the 1880s has been attributed to the net effect of immigration. In recent years, as the birth rate of native-born Americans has slowed, the continuing net movement of legal immigrants to the United States has accounted for more than one third of the population increase.

This trend is important to educators for two reasons. First, it affects school planning. Because immigration has initial, direct, and greatest demographic impact at the state and local levels, high rates of immigration have had a dramatic impact on educational and other social institutions. The majority of newcomers live in urban areas, and nearly three quarters of the 20 million foreign-born residents counted in the 1990 U.S. census resided in one of six states: California, New York, Florida, Texas, New Jersey, or Illinois. California, a traditional destination for immigrants from Asia and Latin America, was home to one third of the foreign-born population.

Second, current immigration trends also indicate particular acculturation patterns of immigrant children through intergenerational transition. Immigrant children have been learning their home cultures— language, values, worldviews, and social knowledge—from parents and others in the home communities; this is enculturation. On immigrating, these children and their parents must acculturate; they must both acquire sufficient knowledge of the new culture to survive. English acquisition and native language attrition or retention are examples of acculturation—adaptation to a new, unfamiliar culture. The foreign-born population usually speaks a language other than English as a first language and retains fairly close ties with native countries and immigrant communities. The second generation, the children of immigrants, has historically been crucial for adaptation to American society. This generation is bilingual and bicultural. They may speak very fluent English, and many of them speak their parents' languages at home. In contrast, the third generation are usually monolingual English speakers. These patterns also have grave implications for services sought from the public schools.

Changes in Racial Composition

Immigration has always been a major force in changing the racial and ethnic composition of the U.S. population. Ethnicity and race of newcomers have changed over time, and this affects the ethnic and racial composition of what are regarded as minority groups. Gradually, it changes the racial and ethnic composition of the population as a whole. Recent immigration has precipitated current shifts in racial and ethnic composition. Until the 1950s, a variety of ethnic groups and nationalities entered the United States, but almost all were white Europeans. Beginning in the 1950s, the composition of immigrants began to change. These shifts were accelerated by changes in U.S. immigration law in the 1960s. Immigration accounts for much of the growth in the minority population. In the past 30 years, more than 75% of all immigrants entering the United States have been from Asian, Hispanic, and black groups. During the 1980s, immigration accounted for half of the growth among Hispanics and nearly three quarters of the growth among Asian Americans. Immigration from Africa and the Caribbean accounted for about one sixth of the U.S. black population growth during the 1980s (Passel & Edmonston, 1992).

A quarter of the current Hispanic population, 5.5 million persons, came from immigration in the 1980s and another 18% from the 1970s. Today, Mexico sends more immigrants to the United States than any other country. Three million Mexicans immigrated to the United States legally during the 1980s and early 1990s, accounting for more than one fourth of all legal immigration.

The Asian population shows a pattern similar to the Hispanic, but with a more overwhelming impact in the most recent cohorts. In spite of the history since the 1840s of immigration from Asia to the United States, the most recent immigrant cohorts have had the greatest effects. About half of the current Asian American population is attributable to immigration in the past 20 years. Asian immigration expanded from 6% of total legal immigration in the 1950s to 44% in the 1980s, 2.6 million Asians. The number is slightly higher than Hispanic immigrants who account for 40%, or 2.4 million, of the legal immigrants in the 1980s. When undocumented immigrants are included, however, Hispanic immigration does surpass Asian immigration for the 1980s.

The pattern for blacks is very different. Immigration since 1900 has had minimal impact on the growth of the black population in the 20th century, which consists almost entirely of descendants of slaves. Thus, only about 8% of the 1990 self-identified black population of 30 million can be attributed to post-1900 immigration (Passel & Edmonston, 1992).

The History of Immigration and Immigrants' Schooling in the United States

Immigration has had enormous effects on the U.S. economy and society. Social responses to new immigrants are a major determinant of the future of race relations. The incorporation of each wave of immigrants and their children challenges American society, and response to this challenge depends on how the children of the newest Americans move through the U.S. educational pipeline. Throughout U.S. history, the country has experienced immigration fluctuations and changes. Although each situation has been different from the others, they have also shared some similarities. A review of previous peaks and troughs of immigration flowing into the United States provides historical perspective on contemporary trends. Comparing current trends with past trends suggests future changes in the racial and ethnic composition of the population and sheds light on the ability of U.S. schools to accommodate such changes.

The Immigration Movement in U.S. History

The number of immigrants to the United States has fluctuated with economic conditions here and abroad, and with U.S. immigration policies. Scholars have argued that these various factors combined to create four major waves of immigration, the first three marked by a peak followed by a trough and the fourth wave being the current one.

The first wave of immigrants arrived between 1790 and 1820 and consisted of mostly English-speaking immigrants from the British Isles (Martin & Midgley, 1994). The second wave, dominated by Irish and German settlers in 1849 and the 1850s, challenged the dominance of

Protestantism and led to a backlash against Catholics and immigrants. The third wave, between 1880 and 1914, brought more than 20 million foreigners to the United States. Most of these were southern and eastern Europeans who found manufacturing jobs in large cities. Immigration in the 20th century was interrupted first by World War I and then in the 1920s by numerical country quotas designed to maintain the dominance of northern Europeans in the country's ethnic balance. The Great Depression and World War II further suppressed immigration flows in the 1930s and 1940s. The fourth and current wave of migration began with immigration reforms in 1965 that eliminated country-by-country quotas.

Changes in U.S. immigration law over time shape and reshape the immigration movement and construct and reconstruct the racial and ethnic composition of immigrants by imposing restrictions on certain people. These restrictions are imposed by establishing national origin quotas because their countries of origin are regarded unfavorably. Until 1890, immigrants from northern and western Europe predominated, but by the turn of the century, the majority of immigrants came from eastern, central, and southern Europe. The Chinese Exclusion Act of 1882, the Gentlemen's Agreement of 1908, and the 1924 Oriental Exclusion Act reduced immigration from Asian countries to a minimum. The Immigration Act of 1924 greatly reduced the total number of immigrants and established quotas that favored northern and western European migration and prevented the entrance of Asian immigrants.

This pattern was broken when the McCarran-Walter Act of 1952, and especially the Immigration Act of 1965, opened up large-scale immigration from the Third World. The act of 1965 abolished the national-origin quotas, and each country was put on a relatively equal footing with a limit of 20,000 immigrants annually. Under the 1965 law, immigrants received priority to enter the United States if they had family ties or if they possessed wanted skills. The 1965 reforms increased the number of immigrants and shifted the countries of origin from Europe to Asia and Latin America. Since then, the main flow of legal immigration has been from Asia and Latin America, but a large influx of undocumented immigrants has occurred from Mexico, the Caribbean, and many other countries throughout the world. Table 1.1 illustrates these historical trends. Hispanic, Asian, and African immigrants accounted only for about 4% of the total U.S. foreign-born population in 1880, about 11% in 1950, but 75% in 1990. Immigration laws of 1986 and 1990 have left standing policy toward countries of origin for legal immigrants.

TABLE 1.1 Percentage of Foreign-Born Population by Region
of Origin: United States, 1880-1990

	1880	1920	1950	1980	1990
Europeans	97.0	93.6	89.3	49.6	25.0
Asians	1.6	1.7	2.6	18.0	25.0
Latin Americans	1.3	4.2	6.3	31.0	43.0
Africans	0.2	0.4	1.8	1.4	7.0

NOTE: Data for 1880, 1920, and 1950 come from U.S. Bureau of the Census
(1975). Data for 1980 come from U.S. Bureau of the Census (1985). Data for
1990 come from U.S. Bureau of the Census (1993b).

These historical patterns place the present experience in context.
Table 1.2 indicates that contemporary immigration, although large, has
a smaller impact relative to population size than previous waves of immigration. Immigration in earlier decades had a larger relative effect.
Although the immigration level of 1900-1910 is similar to the level of
1980-1990, the population of the United States in 1900 was less than one
third the 1990 level of roughly 250 million. Thus, net immigration as a
percentage of population was significantly greater in the early 20th century than it is today. Table 1.2 shows that immigrants and their children
accounted for almost half the U.S. population in 1900 and a third of the
U.S. population in 1920, but less than one fifth the population in 1990.
Nevertheless, the current proportion of immigrants has nearly reached
levels set in the 1930s (Knight, 1997).

Immigration and Schooling

This section of the chapter provides a historical perspective on the
social response to immigration movements and a descriptive review of
educators' ideas and philosophies on how immigrant children should
be educated in the United States. Traditionally, U.S. schools have been
the most important social institution for absorbing newcomers. Few
public institutions have been as directly affected by high levels of immigration as the nation's schools. Urban school districts especially have
been expected to educate large numbers of low-income students, many
with special needs. Today they are also being asked to serve rapidly
increasing numbers of immigrant children, many of whom speak little
or no English. This has never been easy.

TABLE 1.2 Percentage of Foreign Stock in U.S. Population, 1880-1990

	1880	1900	1920	1950	1960	1970	1980	1990
Percentage of foreign born	13.3	13.6	13.2	6.9	5.4	4.7	6.2	8.6
Percentage of foreign or mixed parentage	—	34.3	21.5	16.0	13.6	11.8	9.6	9.7

NOTE: Data for U.S. census of 1880, 1900, 1920, 1950, 1960, and 1970 come from U.S. Bureau of the Census (1900, 1923, 1933, 1953, 1963, 1973, 1975). Data for 1980 from U.S. Bureau of the Census (1981). Data for 1990 from Edmonston and Passel (1992).

Two basic arguments frame the issues in immigrant children's schooling. They center on recruitment of the young to U.S. society— how to be an American—and on the primacy assigned to English instruction. Two prescriptions for the education of immigrants in U.S. society have been put forward over the past century: assimilation and pluralism or multiculturalism. The assimilationist aims at eliminating ethnic boundaries, whereas the pluralist or multiculturalist aims at accommodating them (cf. Cornbleth & Waugh, 1995; Phelan & Davidson, 1993).

Throughout the history of American immigration, a consistent thread has been the fear that the "alien element" would somehow sabotage the institutions of the country and lead them down the path of disintegration. Playing on these nativist fears, the extreme assimilationists have directed heated rhetoric and money to combating these alleged alien elements of evil (Portes & Rumbaut, 1996).

In the late 19th century, the nation was perceived as threatened by increasing immigration from southern, central, and eastern Europe. These new immigrants were thought by many to be too alien and backward to adapt to the United States. Nevertheless, the new immigrants increased and prospered as did their children and grandchildren (cf. Handlin, 1951; Howe, 1980). The adaptation of these new immigrants and their descendants has reached the point where U.S. culture now rests comfortably in the hands of what were considered the "alien" influences of the wave of immigrants from 1880 to 1920 (Portes & Rumbaut, 1996).

Strongly influenced by the educational philosopher Ellwood Cubberley early in the 20th century, the nation's schools took a hard line in the years during and immediately following World War I in seeking the assimilation of the new immigrants from southern and eastern Europe. Cubberley (1909) believed that Americanization required breaking up immigrant groups or settlements, assimilating and amalgamating these peoples as part of an American "race," and implanting in their children the Anglo-Saxon conceptions of righteousness, law and order, public decency, and popular government. The communal nature and cultural habits of many of the regional, ethnic, and religious communities in the United States meant little in Cubberley's vision of a truly "Americanized" America. In Cubberley's view, immigrants were passive, usually illiterate, servile, and often lacking in initiative; their coming had weakened the national breed and was threatening the virtue of American politics and government. Given this crass definition of the problem, a kind of ruthless assimilation was prescribed so as to preserve "our national character." Employers and even YMCAs and other community agencies followed Cubberley's lead (Stewart, 1993). So-called "citizenship education" was an attempt to indoctrinate Anglo-Saxon and Protestant values into these immigrants.

The pluralists' insistence on maintaining group identity, on the other hand, limits the freedom of individuals to choose their own loyalties. It assumes that ethnic boundaries remain fixed and overlooks the divisions within ethnic groups. This view also ignores historical evidence that, in an open, heterogeneous society such as the United States, people work, make friends, and marry outside their ancestral communities (Martin & Midgley, 1994).

Nevertheless, neither assimilation nor pluralism have been realized in the United States. Although extreme assimilation preaches a rejection of one's roots and a disdain for whatever immigrants cannot change or disguise in themselves, ethnic affiliation often persists among the second and third generations of Americans, long after the language and knowledge of the "old country" have been lost (Farrell, 1980).

The assimilation versus pluralism debate is played out in many facets of American life. U.S. public education, however, has strongly rejected conserving and maintaining the native language and cultural values of immigrant children.

Americanization in curriculum and instruction, aimed at socializing immigrants to the norms of the dominant culture, can be traced to the country's genesis. The objective then and in the early years of the federal period was indoctrination—achieving unity through homogeneity.

Today's situation, however, is different from that of a century ago. Sixty years ago, President Herbert Hoover dismissed New York Congressman Fiorella La Guardia, an Italian American, by claiming that "the Italians are predominantly our murderers and bootleggers"; Hoover recommended that La Guardia "go back to where you belong" because "like a lot of other foreign spawn, you do not appreciate this country, which supports you and tolerates you" (Martin & Midgley, 1994, p. 19). Fortunately, this kind of statement from politicians or policymakers is regarded today as repugnant. The structural factors and contexts of immigration today are different from those of the past. Changes have occurred in the political, judicial, international, and social realms in recent years that have modified the process for the better. The demand for the preservation of native languages and cultures is stronger, the arguments for this preservation are better established, and the alliances among immigrant communities and local or national political leaders are more powerful. Many people recognize that diversity is not weakness but strength, and much research conducted in the past several decades has demonstrated the benefits of bilingual and bicultural approaches for immigrant children's education and later careers.

U.S. schools have always been in a difficult situation: providing education and other aids to immigrant children to integrate these children fully and rapidly into U.S. society (Montero-Sieburth & LaCelle-Peterson, 1991). When integration becomes anglicization, however, schools are likely to get into battles with immigrant parents and communities, especially when the loss of native languages and cultures is involved. Accommodation has never been easy or trouble free for immigrants or U.S. schools. Educators struggle to reach some philosophical consensus for policy making and battle for the financing and other resources to support their efforts. Moreover, school plans, curriculum changes, and out-reach actions often are criticized by both advocates and restrictionists. Immigrant advocates believe that U.S. schools have failed to meet immigrant children's special needs; their dissatisfaction is represented by lawsuits that almost every city has pending, charging inadequate and inappropriate language services provided for immigrant students by local government. In many restrictionists' views, however, schools have already succumbed to immigrant communities' demands, jeopardizing the English acquisition of these children as well as the unity and cultural identity of local communities.

Many of today's desperately poor refugees and illegal immigrants do need to learn basic survival skills to cope in U.S. society, and the needs of these immigrants are often very different from those of the native born and from the earlier waves of immigrants from Europe. The core of the challenge of contemporary immigration is that a large percentage of newly arrived immigrants demand sophisticated multicultural curricula and bilingual instruction. School systems may be required to provide bilingual and bicultural education and counseling, as well as English-as-a-second-language (ESL) programs for both children and adults. Unfortunately, teachers and administrators may lack the training, space, and budget to accommodate the needs of so diverse a group of students. Generally speaking, rural and suburban districts are being forced to make difficult changes and adjustments, but they have the capacity to cope and adapt to the challenges posed by immigration. The greatest difficulties are reported in already stressed urban school districts that must find ways to serve both immigrants and the native-born from a diminishing resource base. Overcrowded classrooms, heightened social tensions, fierce controversy over curriculum, and inferior instruction have been the result (McDonnell & Hill, 1993).

Thus far, we have compared contemporary concerns to the response to immigration in the early days when the foreign born represented up to 21% of the American labor force—compared to only 9% in 1990—and close to half the urban population. We have summarized the school situation then and now. The United States is hardly more fragmented now than then; we believe that what held the country together then and continues to do so today is not a coerced cultural homogeneity, but the strength of its political institutions and the durable framework that they offer for diversity, ethnic reaffirmation, and social mobility (Portes & Rumbaut, 1996). The past, however, cannot provide a blueprint for the future. The size and nature of today's immigration require different ways of accommodating newcomers. As the nation searches for a responsible immigration policy for the 21st century, the United States is likely to remain the world's major destination for many immigrants. In Chapter 2, we turn to a consideration of the nature of the children of these immigrants, their families, and their communities.

2

Families and
Communities

In this chapter we identify who the immigrant children are. Despite the educational demands on many school districts with large numbers of immigrants, serious concerns remain about existing policies for immigrant children's schooling. Immigrant students have limited visibility in government documentation at all levels because neither federal nor state educational agencies count immigrants as a separate group. If these children have other characteristics such as limited English proficiency (LEP), a learning or physical disability, giftedness, or other social disadvantage, they are counted as part of these other groups. Furthermore, for most policymakers, immigrant education is focused on helping students learn English, and immigrant education policy is essentially English language acquisition policy. McDonnell and Hill (1993) have reported that every state policymaker they interviewed, regardless of role, position, or political ideology, equated the two. They claim that limited policy is the product of both judicial and legislative actions—the mandatory requirement of aiding LEP students—although many may agree that educating immigrant children should include a wide range of services.

Planning and implementing a variety of services for immigrant children has obvious problems—cognitive, psychological, and technical. The limited visibility of immigrant students and narrowly defined school policies are often indications of educators' lack of reliable estimates of immigrant student numbers, lack of awareness of their social and demographic characteristics, and ignorance of their special needs. To develop and implement a sound policy for educating immigrant children, we must acknowledge and understand the immigration experience, and we must have accurate and timely information about immigration trends and about the characteristics of immigrant students locally and nationally.

To address these concerns, we provide an updated demographic profile of U.S. immigrant students aged 5-18. Because we use a cultural-contextual interactive model to examine immigrant education, we include information whenever possible on children's surroundings—the social and physical environments in which immigrant children live, related information on immigrant adults, the types of families in which children live, residential neighborhoods, local communities, and the states and regions in which they live. Information on their language resources, the attrition and retention of their native tongues, and English acquisition is introduced in Chapter 3.

We have used a combination of data sources for this analysis: census data, data collected by the National Center for Educational Statistics, data from other sources, and information cited in the research literature. The most comprehensive and up-to-date information comes from the 1990 census, including aggregated data and individual data. We show similarities and differences between native-born children and immigrant children, contrast immigrant adults and children, compare immigrant groups, and suggest what these patterns mean for educators.

A Demographic Profile of Immigrant Children Aged 5-18 and Immigrant Adults

In this section, we draw a sketch of immigrant children aged 5-18 in the United States. Like any sketch—selective in its hues, strokes, focus, and perspective—it is likely to be imperfect and incomplete because it is a representation of a subject too rich and elusive to be rendered in a single image. Because our nation periodically erupts in public debate over newcomers and their effect on the social fabric, we educators must separate myth from reality, perception from fact, and the benefits from the costs of immigration.

Immigrant Adults

If we want to know about immigrant children, it is important to know about the environments in which they grow up, that is, their families and communities. General information about immigrant adults helps us know the contextual background for the foreign-born children. Our main sources for the information in this section are *The Foreign-Born Population: 1994* (Hansen & Bachu, 1995), *We the American Foreign Born* (Lapham, 1993), and other publications that use data published by the U.S. Bureau of the Census. This information, deriving from 1990 census data and the 1994 *Current Population Report*, presents a mosaic of social and cultural characteristics of American new immigrants.

We first provide a demographic profile for these immigrant adults and a socioeconomic profile thereafter. Like pictures that are variable and colorful in a kaleidoscope, these profiles change with the year of entry, the length of residency, country of origin, and their interplay.

About half of the current U.S. foreign-born population arrived after 1980, and 20% of them—about 5 million persons—reached this land in the 5-year period between 1990 and 1994. Of the 22.7 million foreign born living in the United States in March 1994, 6.2 million came from Mexico. Among the top 10 sending countries, Mexico was the country of origin with the largest number of immigrants. More than one million Filipinos are the next largest group. Other countries sending the most immigrants are Cuba (805,000), El Salvador (718,000), Canada (679,000), Germany (625,000), China (565,000), the Dominican Republic (556,000), Vietnam (496,000), and India (494,000).

Although the median age of all foreign-born persons in the United States (37 years) is higher than the median age for natives (33 years), age and year of entry are interconnected. Among foreign-born groups, Mexicans, Salvadorans, and Vietnamese had the youngest population with median ages of less than 30. Italian, Canadian, and German immigrants had the highest median ages of over 50. The most recent immigrants, those who entered the United States between 1990 and 1994, have a median age of only 26 years. Foreign-born women have a higher birth rate (1.5 children each) than native-born women (1.2 children each). No connections appear between fertility and year of entry, but there is a suggested association between education and year of entry.

We now move to the socioeconomic profile of immigrant adults. Although it seems a paradox, as we have noted previously, the foreign born are both more educated and less educated than natives. Among people 25 years and over, recent immigrants are more likely to have a college degree than either natives or earlier immigrants. Although 11.5% of recent immigrants have a graduate or professional degree, only about 7.5% of native-born people and immigrants in earlier years have such a degree. Recent immigrants are also more likely to have bachelor's degrees (21%) than either natives (14.7%) or earlier immigrants (13.9%). On the other hand, immigrants are also less likely to have graduated from high school than natives. Of immigrants, 65% have high school degrees compared to 83% of natives. A great variation in educational attainment occurs between and within nationality groups. The 1990 census data indicate that Filipinos have the highest high school graduate rates (83%), and Mexicans have the lowest (24.3%). Although the percentage of Chinese with a bachelor's degree is about 50% higher than the native-born population, the percentage of Chinese without a high school degree is more than 50% higher than the native born.

The economic condition of foreign-born persons significantly improves with the length of their residence in the United States. Foreign-born persons in general had a lower median income in 1993 than natives ($12,179 vs. $15,876), but this difference is related to length of residence. Recent immigrants have the lowest median income ($8,393) of all immigrants, but immigrants who are citizens have median incomes ($16,103) slightly higher than that of natives. Median family income varies widely by country of birth. In 1989, the median income for families headed by a foreign-born person was $31,785 compared with $35,225 for all U.S. families. The median income for families with a household head born in the Philippines was $47,794, but median incomes among heads of household born in El Salvador and Mexico were the lowest at $21,585 and $21,818, respectively. In the United States, families maintained by a female with no husband present usually had lower median incomes than all families. This is also true among foreign-born families across nationalities. Families with foreign-born heads of female households, however, generally had a higher median income than for U.S. female-headed families, $18,860 versus $17,414, respectively. The median family income for female-headed families of Philippine origin was $32,817; of Italian, $28,483; of Canadian, $26,500; of United Kingdom, $26,071; and of Chinese, $25,556. All were about 50% higher than that of native-born female-headed families.

Length of residency affects the immigrant's economic well-being in home ownership as well. Although persons who immigrated before 1970 have homeownership rates (77%) higher than natives (69%), only

18% of recent immigrants are living in their own homes. The foreign born as a whole are 1.6 times more likely to be living in poverty than natives (22.9% vs. 14.4%). Although persons who immigrated prior to 1970 are less likely than natives to be classified as poor (10.8%), recent immigrants are more than 2.5 times as likely to be living in poverty (37%) as native born. Recent immigrants are more likely than natives to receive public assistance income (5.7% vs. 2.9%). The rates drop significantly for immigrants who have been in the United States 5 or more years. Public assistance rates for immigrants who have lived in the United States for 5 years or longer are not significantly different from those of natives, and immigrants who arrived before 1970 are less likely to be receiving public assistance (1.4%) than natives. The foreign-born population has a higher unemployment rate than do natives (9% vs. 7%, respectively), especially among foreign-born persons who are not citizens (10.7% unemployment rate). Most of them are recent immigrants.

A greater proportion of foreign born, both male and female, are employed as blue-collar workers and service workers, and foreign-born individuals are less likely than native-born people to be managers and professional workers. Occupational distribution, however, varies by country of origin. Although people from Great Britain (40%), Canada (38%), Germany (33%), China (29%), the Philippines (28%), and Korea (25.5%) are more likely to be managers and professional workers than the native born (25.5%), those from Mexico (6%), El Salvador (15.5%), Vietnam (17%), Italy (20%), and Cuba (23.5%) are less likely to be in this category than the native born.

The socioeconomic condition of Salvadoran and Vietnamese immigrants demonstrates the relationship between years of entry, length of residency, and economic well-being of the foreign born. Salvadorans and Vietnamese are the youngest large immigrant groups in the United States: About 80% of Salvadorans and 65% of Vietnamese arrived after 1980. They have lower median family incomes, higher unemployment rates, and a higher percentage of families below the poverty level (25% for Salvadorans and 26% for Vietnamese) than other nationality groups who came to the United States earlier and hence are better established.

Of the foreign-born population in the United States, 31% are naturalized citizens. The rates at which immigrants from various countries have naturalized varies considerably. According to Martin and Midgley (1994), distance to the United States and the affiliation of countries of origin with the United States are two of the most influential factors on naturalization rates. People who have migrated from a long distance and people who have fled their countries for political reasons have the highest rates of naturalization. In contrast, people from countries historically and geographically closest to the United States have the lowest rates of naturalization. For example, of the Canadians and Mexicans admitted with immigration visas from 1970 to 1979, fewer than one in six had become citizens by 1992. Most immigrants from western European countries also tend not to take American citizenship. Four of five Vietnamese and almost two of three Filipino and Chinese immigrants arriving between 1970 and 1979, however, had become U.S. citizens by 1992.

In summary, although recent changes in immigration trends and variations among immigrant groups can be observed, the socioeconomic status of immigrants, especially the newest comers, is generally lower than that of natives. Many recent immigrants belonged to the middle and upper classes in their countries of origin, but most could not bring property with them under harsh conditions of emigration or under home governmental policy prohibiting or restricting emigrants from transporting money or other property to other countries. A census monograph compiled by Taeuber and Taeuber (1971) reports that revolution and instability, war and persecution, flight and displacement have been important factors in the decisions of individuals to migrate. Some of the new immigrants had advanced education in their home countries, but their professional credentials have not always been recognized in the new homeland. Language difficulties and the absence of work experience in the new country are factors that lead to lower income for and underemployment of many recent immigrant workers. As a consequence, they are more likely to be living under the poverty level and eligible for public assistance. Immigrants who have been in the United States for some years, however, and are therefore better established do better economically, occupationally, and educationally than the native born. Census data overwhelmingly indicate that, after overcoming initial difficulties, immigration to the United States benefits immigrants themselves and the receiving communities as well.

As the data suggest, schools should make distinctions among the various groups based on these factors and recognize the special needs of the immigrant communities they serve. Because they are one of the most important social institutions, schools must help integrate recent immigrant parents into the broader community through adult literacy programs and immigration information centers set up in some schools, just as they integrate students into newcomer programs and social adjustment classes. These programs promote understanding of the host society and its major institutions and therefore help adults adjust to the new society. As a result, their children's schooling benefits.

A Demographic Profile of
Immigrant Children Aged 5-18

A demographic profile of foreign-born children who are school aged is useful to the nation's educators. First, as mentioned previously, government at all levels has not kept any official records for foreign-born students as a separate group. The data we have compiled, summarized, and reported in this section are indispensable national representations of immigrant children in the United States. Second, changes in immigration trends and patterns in the past three decades have devastated schools and other institutions that offer services to large numbers of immigrant children, partially because their policies are based on outdated information. Timely and accurate data can help schools shift their priorities; reallocate budgets; restaff their faculty and other school personnel; and adjust and reinvent their curricula, teaching materials, and other resources. Census data do, however, have weaknesses for studies of this kind. Recent immigrant families, particularly those who are poor, who do not have permanent addresses, who are undocumented, and who speak and read no English, are the ones who are least represented because of census undercount problems (see Sources of Information)

As we have been emphasizing, U.S. schools have faced the challenge of educating students with foreign backgrounds for more than a century. According to the 1880 census data, one of every three persons aged 5-20 was either foreign born or had one or two foreign parents. The figure has gradually declined, but it is still high—about one in six in 1990. A 1990 estimate indicates that 16%-18% of 50 million pupils in elementary and secondary schools are first- or second-generation immigrants. This number suggests that 9 million children, including undocumented immigrant children, in U.S. public schools are either foreign born or have a parent who is foreign born.

Recent immigration not only changes the generational composition of the U.S. student population, but also transforms its racial and ethnic composition. Figure 2.1 contrasts the patterns of the racial and ethnic composition of foreign-born children and native-born children in 1990. Although three of four native-born children are non-Hispanic white, only one of six foreign-born children are non-Hispanic white. The pro-

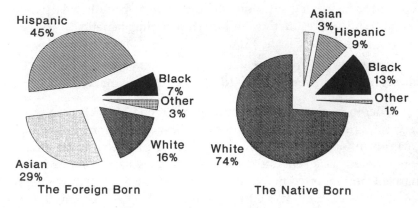

Figure 2.1. Race-Ethnic Composition of Native-Born and Foreign-Born Children, U.S., 1990

SOURCE: U.S. Bureau of the Census (1993b).

portion of Hispanic children among the foreign born is six times the proportion of Hispanics in the native-born population (45% vs. 9%), and the same pattern occurs among Asian children (29% among the foreign born vs. 3% among the native born).

Among 15- to 18-year-old foreign-born children, the largest group is Mexican-born children: 550,000 account for a quarter of this category. Countries rounding out the top 10 are 100,000 Chinese children (4.5% of the foreign born); 80,000 Vietnamese children (3.7%); 77,000 Italian children (3.5%); 76,000 Filipino children (3.4%); 63,000 Korean children (2.9%); 61,000 Salvadoran children (2.8%); 37,000 Asian Indian children (1.7%); 36,000 Dominican children (1.6%); and 29,000 Jamaican children (1.3%). The remaining half come from various other countries.

By 1990, 9 of 10 foreign-born children aged 5-18 had arrived in the United States between 1980 and 1990: more than half had arrived between 1985 and 1990 and one third of those arrived between 1987 and 1990. Foreign-born children are older than native children. Figure 2.2 presents the gap in the ages between these two groups. Of the children aged 5-18 years old, only 33% of the foreign born were 5-10 years old, but 45% of native-born children fell in that age range. The same data also indicate that more foreign-born youth than native-born youth fell in the age group between 14 and 18 years (47% vs. 34%).

Analysis of living arrangements shows 78% of 5- to 18-year-old foreign-born children lived with parents or adopted parents, 4% lived

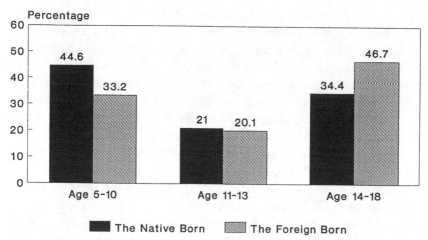

Figure 2.2. The Age Composition of Native-Born and Foreign-Born Children, U.S., 1990

SOURCE: U.S. Bureau of the Census (1993b).

with siblings, and 7% lived with other relatives. The percentage of children not living with parents in 1990 was higher among the foreign born than the native born. This gap is largest for the 17- to 18-year-old group: 75% of native-born youth lived with parents versus 60% of foreign-born youth. Data on family type reveal that 71% of foreign-born children lived with two parents, 14% lived in female-headed households, and 7% lived in male-headed households. The percentage of foreign-born children living with a parent but not living with both parents during 1990 was slightly higher than that of native-born children (27% to 25%). Enormous cross-group variation occurred, however: 83% of non-Hispanic white, 81% of Asian, 71% of Hispanic, and 56% of African children were living with two parents, the percentage ranging as high as 93% for foreign-born Japanese children and as low as 48% for Dominican children.

The demographic profile of immigrant children suggests many policy-related issues for U.S. schools. For example, many inner-city schools that serve large numbers of immigrant students may need to reset their priorities when they consider serving minority students. The 1990 census data clearly reveal that the newcomers to our schools are Mexican and Asian children. Almost all school-aged foreign-born children who lived in urban areas had been in this country less than 10 years in 1990. One of every two foreign-born children in the United States has been here less than 5 years, and one of three has been in this country less than 3 years. Social, language, and schooling adjustments for these children must be addressed quickly, because about half of these children are high-school aged (14-18). Learning English speedily may be hampered because they are grappling with new vocabulary and knowledge in reading assignments in all subjects, especially in science and social studies. They must also adjust to U.S.-style schooling and school social life, including peer pressure and the antischool culture typically formed in U.S. inner-city schools (e.g., Fordham, 1996).

As some scholars have indicated, although immigrants revitalize U.S. inner cities, U.S. inner-city schools serve a disproportion of both immigrant minority students and native-born minority students who come from low-socioeconomic backgrounds. Immigrant children who live in inner cities are more likely to live with one parent or other relatives. They are the most recent immigrants, noncitizens, and poor. The long-distance migration and differences in the physical environments of home countries and the United States leave many children exhausted and sick. Some also suffer from emotional stress due to the harsh experiences in their homelands or during the immigration journey. Many children who enter the United States have to endure family separations in the course of immigration. In many cases, even intact families are frequently disrupted by parents' emotional distress and their need to work multiple jobs. Schooling routines may be interrupted by journeys back and forth between the homeland and the United States or by frequent school transfers. The foreign born move more frequently than the native born, especially recent immigrants and the poor, who are more likely to move from town to town and state to state for financial reasons and employment opportunities (McDonnell & Hill, 1993).

Spatial Mobility,
Spatial Concentration, and U.S. Schools

Apart from annual fluctuations of immigrants to the United States, the two major changes in immigration trends in this century are changes in the countries of immigrants' origin and the distributive homogeneity of the immigrant population. We have discussed the first major change in Chapter 1 and in the first part of this chapter. We focus on the second major change in the following section, a trend toward patterns of both more clustering and more relatively widespread distribution. This section provides material useful for educational planners, educational administrators, and local governments, alerting schools to the newcomers they will receive in the next several decades—who the immigrants are and how schools can help them. It examines the spatial concentration and spatial mobility of immigrants—immigrants' geographic movement inside the United States.

Although U.S. schools have always had to meet the challenge of educating newcomers, the difficulties have varied by area. Areas previously having low proportions of immigrants now show increases (Alatis & Staczek, 1985). Among states that traditionally have had few immigrants, all now have a considerable immigrant population, and areas that once had considerable numbers of immigrants now show a visible immigrant population decline. Recent census figures show that Asians and Hispanics are beginning to disperse more widely throughout the country, in some instances quite far from the places to which they originally immigrated.

Spatial Mobility: Clusters, Networks, and Ethnic Enclaves

In this section, we discuss the patterns of how immigrants settle and why they move. The concentration of the immigrant population, especially populations of people from the same region or same ethnic group, is widely recognized. Immigrant concentrations relate to entry, initial settlement, and secondary migration. Therefore, we begin very briefly with movement and disparity, clusters, and ethnic enclaves, taking into account other variables that affect patterns of immigrant settlement, such as race, ethnicity, country of origin, length of entry, and socioeconomic status.

Historically, most immigrants have been concentrated in a handful of states, and that pattern continues. The residential distribution of immigrants at any point in time is a function of their initial distribution on entry to the United States and secondary migration within the United States. Given the historical residential preferences of the foreign born, questions arise about the geographic distribution of the new immigrants and other variables (Neuman & Tienda, 1994).

Using microdata from the 1980 census, Bartel (1989) observed higher rates of internal migration among the foreign-born compared to the native-born population. One reason immigrants may move more than natives is that they may have shallower social ties in their initial U.S. destinations. This suggests a duration dependence between length of U.S. residence and the propensity to move, with earlier arrivals exhibiting higher propensities to move than later arrivals. The better educated immigrants move long distances for better opportunities, and the least educated move locally and only because they must.

The well-established positive association between education and internal migration reflects both a greater willingness on the part of the better educated to take risks and their enhanced ability to evaluate the costs and benefits of a move. Bartel (1989) found that better educated immigrants have higher rates of migration and that their geographic movement reduces spatial concentration, despite the absence of a tendency toward dispersion among the foreign-born population as a whole. The best-educated immigrants are most likely to disperse, and the least educated are most likely to cluster. The concentration of immigrants from the same region or even the same country serves as a network providing immigrants with job information and employment opportunities. The neighborhood residential cluster also may enhance ethnic group identity, hence increasing immigrants' sense of security and helping them to resist racial discrimination. These immigrant-ethnic clusters are usually called ethnic enclaves, also viewed as a form of neighborhood segregation, reflecting housing problems and social and racial dissonance.

Neuman and Tienda (1994) found differences among country-origin groups. Asian immigrants were more likely to engage in secondary migration than either Europeans or Hispanics. In addition, they found that secondary migration resulted in a greater spatial concentration of foreign born, although this varied somewhat by origin groups. Movers from Asia have become more concentrated than nonmovers. Movers from Mexico and El Salvador and other Latin American, African, and European countries become less residentially concentrated than their fellow ethnics who stay in their state of entry.

State Concentrations

The foreign-born population is distributed unevenly throughout the country. Not surprisingly, Table 2.1 shows that the five states that historically host the majority of immigrants—California, New York, New Jersey, Illinois, and Massachusetts—still hold the majority of current immigrants.

TABLE 2.1 Distribution of Foreign-Born Population Among the
States: U.S., 1880-1994 (in percentages)

	1880		1920		1950		1980		1994	
Rank										
1st	NY	18.1	NY	20.2	NY	24.1	CA	25.4	CA	34.0
2nd	PA	8.8	PA	10.0	CA	10.1	NY	17.0	NY	13.0
3rd	IL	8.7	IL	8.7	IL	7.6	FL	7.6	FL	9.2
4th	MA	6.7	MA	7.8	PA	7.5	TX	6.1	TX	8.0
5th	WI	6.1	CA	5.4	MA	6.9	IL	5.9	NJ	4.8
6th	OH	5.9	NJ	5.3	NJ	6.1	NJ	5.4	IL	4.8
7th	MI	5.8	MI	5.2	MI	5.8	MA	3.6	MA	2.6
Remainder states		39.9		37.4		31.9		29.0		23.6
Total		100.0		100.0		100.0		100.0		100.0

NOTE: Data for 1880, 1920, 1950, and 1980 come from U.S. Bureau of the Census (1900, 1923, 1953, 1963, 1973, 1975, 1983a). Data for 1994 come from Hansen and Bachu (1995).

Among these, the foreign born remain concentrated in two states. According to the most recent estimates, in 1994 about half of the nation's legal and illegal immigrants lived in California or New York (Hansen & Bachu, 1995). For many decades New York State was home to about a fifth of the nation's immigrants. California surpassed New York in the 1970s and now contains more than a third of the foreign born. California is now home to 7.7 million foreign-born persons— more than one third of all immigrants to the United States and nearly one quarter of all California residents. New York ranks second with 2.9 million. Two southern states now lead most northeastern states in becoming homes to newcomers. Florida ranks third with 2.1 million foreign born, and Texas ranks fourth with 1.8 million foreigners. Two other states have more than 1 million foreign-born residents—Illinois, and New Jersey (Hansen & Bachu, 1995).

This information indicates a new trend. States such as Pennsylvania and Michigan used to share a larger percentage of immigrants (5%-8% from 1880 through 1960), but their percentage of immigrants decreased to 2% in each state in 1994. The North Central states, which previously accounted for a large percentage of immigrants, have been

TABLE 2.2 Foreign-Born Population and Percentage of 5- to
17-Year-Olds Who Have Problems Speaking English, by
State, U.S., 1990

	Total Population (in thousands)	Foreign-Born Population (in thousands)	Foreign-Born as Percentage of State Population	Foreign-Born as Percentage of U.S. Population	5- to 17-Year-Old Percentage of LEP[a]
All states	248,124	19,724		7.9	37.8
California	29,690	6,463	21.8	32.8	42.4
New York	17,902	2,850	15.9	14.4	35.4
Hawaii	1,106	156	14.1	0.8	38.0
Florida	12,930	1,662	12.9	8.4	31.5
New Jersey	7,579	975	12.9	4.9	31.0
Massachusetts	6,009	567	9.4	2.9	35.1
Texas	16,869	1,511	9.0	7.7	40.2
District of Columbia	598	53	8.9	0.3	42.2
Nevada	1,192	103	8.6	0.5	37.2
Connecticut	3,278	280	8.5	1.4	34.3
Rhode Island	995	85	8.5	0.4	34.4
Illinois	11,176	945	8.5	4.8	33.8
Arizona	3,644	270	7.4	1.4	39.0
Maryland	4,580	309	6.7	1.6	32.2
Washington	4,878	326	6.7	1.7	38.4
New Mexico	1,500	89	5.9	0.5	35.7
Alaska	544	28	5.1	0.1	36.8
Virginia	6,087	310	5.1	1.6	31.7
Oregon	2,837	142	5.0	0.7	35.8
Colorado	3,296	142	4.3	0.7	35.0
New Hampshire	952	40	4.2	0.2	30.2
Michigan	9,275	352	3.8	1.8	29.0
Utah	1,717	61	3.6	0.3	33.1
Pennsylvania	11,781	380	3.2	1.9	36.6
Idaho	1,003	29	2.9	0.1	35.0
Maine	1,128	31	2.7	0.2	26.7
Minnesota	4,048	108	2.7	0.5	40.4
Georgia	6,290	166	2.6	0.8	35.4
Kansas	2,456	62	2.5	0.3	35.2
Vermont	558	14	2.5	0.1	24.1

TABLE 2.2 *Continued*

	Total Population (in thousands)	Foreign-Born Population (in thousands)	Foreign-Born as Percentage of State Population	Foreign-Born as Percentage of U.S. Population	5- to 17-Year-Old Percentage of LEP[a]
Ohio	10,393	254	2.4	1.3	36.4
Wisconsin	4,791	116	2.4	0.6	37.8
Oklahoma	3,118	67	2.1	0.3	33.4
Louisiana	4,187	81	1.9	0.4	34.1
Montana	784	14	1.8	0.7	32.9
Delaware	227	4	1.8	0.0	37.3
Nebraska	1,536	26	1.7	0.1	29.9
North Carolina	6,606	114	1.7	0.6	40.1
Iowa	2,453	39	1.6	0.2	35.6
Indiana	5,430	82	1.5	0.4	36.9
Missouri	5,125	77	1.5	0.4	36.3
South Carolina	3,488	51	1.5	0.3	34.6
Wyoming	459	7	1.5	0.0	28.4
North Dakota	537	7	1.3	0.0	25.9
Tennessee	4,678	54	1.2	0.3	33.8
Alabama	3,976	46	1.2	0.2	35.1
South Dakota	696	8	1.1	0.0	33.0
Arkansas	2,124	21	1.0	0.1	31.7
West Virginia	1,398	15	1.0	0.1	30.8
Mississippi	2,511	22	0.9	0.1	37.3
Kentucky	3,463	29	0.8	0.1	37.3

NOTE: Data from U.S. Bureau of the Census (1993a).

a. LEP (limited English proficiency): 5- to 17-year-old foreign-born children who self-reportedly do not speak English very well.

replaced as major attractors by states along the southern boundary: California (34%), Florida (9.2%), and Texas (8%).

Table 2.2 lists the numbers and percentages of immigrants in each of the 50 U.S. states in 1990. It also provides information on the percentage of children aged 5-17 who reportedly lack English proficiency. One of five Californians and one of six New Yorkers and Hawaiians are foreign born. One of 10 people in Florida, Texas, New Jersey, Illinois, Massachusetts, Connecticut, Rhode Island, and Washington, D.C. was born outside the United States. The percentage of the foreign-born population in many southern and western states was nearly zero 100 years ago, but all now have considerable percentages of immigrants in urban areas.

The increasing percentages of the foreign-born population in many states are much higher than those in the general population.

Maryland, Florida, Virginia, Georgia, Texas, New Mexico, Nevada, California, and Alaska have had more than a 50% increase in their foreign populations, and in other states the foreign population also has increased significantly: North Carolina (46%), Washington (36%), Oregon (32%), New Jersey (29%), and Colorado (25%). Meanwhile, most of the central states had a significant decline in their foreign population during 1980-1990.

Table 2.2 also shows that the percentage of 5- to 17-year-old children in the foreign population who lack English proficiency is distributed unevenly among immigrants in various states. Some states, such as Minnesota (2.7% of foreign-born) and North Carolina (1.7% of foreign-born) with moderate percentages of immigrant children, may have among the highest percentages of foreign-born children with problems speaking English, 40.4% for Minnesota and 40.1% for North Carolina.

The shift in the distribution of immigrants has created difficult situations. No state can ignore the immigrant issue; all states require an agenda for educating immigrants or their children. In some states the task has become urgent. For example, more than half of the immigrants entering California come from Spanish-speaking nations (Knight, 1997). This places tremendous strain on the state's bilingual teachers. Similar problems are faced by many other states, especially New York, Texas, and Florida. The southern states may have additional problems in coping with this. In the past three decades, southern Sunbelt states have experienced the highest population growth in the United States, bringing large numbers of native and international migrants into many of their towns and metropolitan areas. The public school systems in these states not only are under pressure from an increase in the general student population, but also are faced with a diversifying student population, including a large portion of immigrants and linguistic minorities. Historically, educators in southeastern states have been the least prepared—psychologically, emotionally, and organizationally—to receive immigrants and to meet their special needs. Many southeastern residents know little about Asian and Hispanic peoples and have had no contact with them in the past. In many areas of the Southeast where the Asian and Hispanic population has doubled or tripled in the past decade, the knowledge and preparation of many educators and policymakers for the education of these children remain negligible (Villenas, 1996).

About 40% of Asian Americans live in California, and Mexican immigrants are concentrated in a few states, with the majority in California. In 1990, California was home to 57% of the 4.4 million Mexican-born U.S. residents. Texas (with 22%) and Illinois (with 7%) were the only other two states with more than 250,000 Mexican-born residents in 1990. These same states also contain most of the Mexican migrants entering illegally. The INS estimates that about 60% of illegal Mexican immigrants resided in California in 1992; the next largest shares lived in Texas (17%) and Illinois (6%).

Urban Concentration

Immigration since the 1960s has facilitated urban renewal by strengthening small business, providing low-wage labor, and maintaining the population base necessary to sustain a high level of economic activity. The new immigrants—unskilled workers, professionals, and entrepreneurs—have encouraged the flow of investment, furnished workers for factories and service industries, and helped revive deteriorating urban neighborhoods (Morse, 1994).

Immigrants and their children, particularly new immigrants and immigrants with less education, however, are likely to be concentrated in big-city school districts already under severe stress. More than one third of the students needing special instruction because of poor English skills are enrolled in one of the country's 47 largest city school districts. These same schools contain a large proportion of low-income and minority pupils: More than half of the students in these schools were eligible for free or reduced-price lunches in 1990, and three quarters of those enrolled were Hispanic, Asian, or African American (Martin & Midgley, 1994). Immigrant children who live in central cities are less likely to have English proficiency than immigrant children who live in the suburbs and in rural areas. Especially among Asian children, 49% who live in central cities reported having problems speaking English versus 36% who live in other places. The percentages are 42% versus 38% for Hispanic children, and 37% versus 35% for black children. The composition of the population of U.S. cities has changed with the influx of immigrants in new proportions, as the following examples illustrate (Morse, 1994).

- Atlanta, GA: During the 1980s, Georgia experienced the most rapid increase of any state in people speaking languages other than English at home—113%. Blacks are Atlanta's largest minority group, comprising one third of the city population of 2.8 million residents. The Asian and Hispanic population, however, grew from 20,000 in 1980 to 200,000 in 1992.
- Miami, FL: Miami's population is almost half Hispanic (60% of them are Cuban) and nearly one fifth black. The population of non-Hispanic whites has declined to 30%. Dade County attributes 95% of its growth in the past decade to the foreign born.
- Lowell, MA: One in seven residents of Lowell is a recent immigrant. Cambodian refugees began arriving in the early 1980s, fleeing war and the Khmer Rouge. By 1985, the community had grown to 3,000 people and established the first Buddhist temple on the east coast, attracting even more Cambodians. Lowell is now home to more than 20,000 Cambodians, about 20% of the city's population.

Other cities that have long neglected serving the special needs of immigrants are experiencing a rapid increase in their foreign-born population, such as Charlotte and Raleigh-Durham in North Carolina, Phoenix, and New Orleans. As we have noted, the 1990 census data on cities reveal that one third to two thirds of immigrant children in cities have problems speaking English. The demands of language service put tremendous pressures on local schools with booming immigrant student populations but with little past experience to take on a task of this kind.

As this information has indicated, state and local policymakers face the need to provide basic services with few resources for communities composed of diverse ethnic and social groups, most of whom are legally resident in the United States. Knowledge of the spatial concentration of immigrant children is useful because the extent of the concentration usually suggests different patterns of school programs for LEP students: In jurisdictions where non-English-speaking populations are larger and better established, the distribution of resources and education programs for immigrant children has been different than where

LEP populations are smaller or newer. Where large groups of speakers of one language are located, such as Spanish-speaking populations in California and Texas, bilingual education is widely used to help keep immigrant children from falling behind in school. In places where a great variety of languages are spoken and no one foreign-language group predominates, as in Fairfax County, Virginia, English-as-a-second-language (ESL) instruction is often the remedy used (McDonnell & Hill, 1993).

Knowledge of movement is also useful to cities and states in making short- and long-term plans, including staffing and resource allocation, both human and material. Although immigrants can be economic and cultural assets, they make demands on state and local governments. In California, newcomers have put a strain on public resources and infrastructure. More than two thirds of all newcomers settle in urban areas. In one school district in New York City, more than 100 languages are spoken. In Minnesota's Twin Cities, a substantial Southeast Asian population is compelling state and local social service delivery systems to accommodate new cultural and religious traditions. In many other states and localities, newcomers put additional demands on scarce public resources as well. These newcomers require health care, education, job training, police and emergency services, social services, and housing.

Furthermore, the effects of rapid transformation on communities can lead to racial and ethnic tensions (Morse, 1994). Public anxieties about the current surge of immigrants are generally economic as well as social, concerns that immigrant enclaves are economically, culturally, and psychologically separate from the mainstream. Recent outbreaks of violence in U.S. cities have led some observers to question whether the nation can continue to absorb large numbers of newcomers without paying a high price in ethnic strife. Many news stories claim that some U.S. large cities have become battlefields between immigrants and native minorities. Newcomers in large cities elicit anxiety and hostility from local native-born minorities more likely to be less educated, poorer, and unemployed than the general minority population. Confrontations are usually caused by a lack of cultural understanding on both sides; competition in the local job market; different political and social perceptions on issues of race, social class, and political ideology—and worst—the mutual discrimination of race and xenophobia. Schools in highly concentrated areas of immigrants can serve as cultural and language brokers for their communities and also can bridge the cultural gap between immigrants and long-established native residents. In doing so, schools can promote equitable and fair treatment for both newcomers and native residents.

Therefore, we believe the policy for educating immigrant children should be defined in a much broader context of the five related dimensions recommended by McDonnell and Hill (1993).

1. It should include a change of course offerings and the adjustment and development of teaching materials by making them more suitable for immigrant students. It must also include modification of conventional instructional strategies and acquisition of needed skills to work with children with little English.
2. It needs to extend the regular curriculum to inform students about how U.S. society differs from their native countries and how to cope with U.S. institutions including schools, occupational opportunities and employment networks, and varied social situations.
3. It is essential to have staff development and to change school staffing by recruiting people with bilingual and bicultural skills or training adequate to accommodate immigrant students' needs.
4. It is necessary to expand educational opportunities for adult immigrants to assist immigrant children by improving the economic status of their families and giving parents skills to enable them to help their children do well in school.
5. Many schools in urban areas are the only places to gather people together. Schools should, if possible, help established residents and immigrant communities know each other by introducing information on new immigrants to the local population.

The task may become more difficult, however, and resolutions have to be more inventive. Although more immigrants are arriving, the federal government has reduced or restricted the few programs that assist new immigrants in integrating into the economic, social, and civic life of the United States. Federal funding for refugees, legalized aliens, and immigrant education programs has been delayed or cut substantially. For the most part, the responsibility for integrating immigrants into society has been left to state and local government, private organizations, and immigrants themselves (Morse, 1994).

3

Overcoming
Language Barriers

Immigration adds students with English language difficulties to the challenges facing American schools. The 1990 census counted slightly more than 2 million foreign-born children under age 18; more than three quarters of them came from countries where English is not the dominant language or the official language. U.S. classrooms include not only foreign-born children, but also U.S.-born children of recent immigrants—many of whom speak languages other than English at home: The census found 6.3 million such children (Martin & Midgley, 1994). Of these, 38% were reported to have difficulty speaking English. In this chapter, however, we focus on foreign-born children only.

Our focus here is the language reality of immigrant children, including acquiring English and the loss or maintenance of bilingualism across ethnic groups. We do not view English learning as an isolated process, equal to learning a technical skill. Instead, we see the acquisition of English, the retention or attrition of native tongues, the linguistic environment (including household languages and the extent to which households are linguistically isolated), the language resources, and the sociocultural environment of the community as interactive. We believe that all links of the process contribute to a child's linguistic adaptation and deserve to be studied as the interplay of the links. Without understanding the whole process, we cannot fully comprehend why some immigrant children learn English more effectively than others.

The loss or maintenance of native language and English adaptation across cohorts who entered the United States in various time periods is also addressed in this chapter, where we examine language adjustment using our cultural-contextual interactive approach. Our bias is that language shifts and English acquisition parallel the history of immigrant adaptation to U.S. culture, society, and economy. According to Portes and Rumbaut (1996), language in the United States—and perhaps in some other nations also—has a meaning broader than the instrumental value of communication. English has become the symbol of commitment to Americanization; acquisition of nonaccented English and dropping of native languages represent the test of an immigrant's patriotism. Language homogeneity has come to be seen as the cornerstone of collective identity. Immigrants have been compelled to speak English well, but also to speak English only, as the prerequisite of their social acceptance and integration. Although this section focuses on the linguistic authenticity of school-aged children among the newest U.S. immigrants, it does not, however, detail the debates over bilingualism or the English-as-the-only-official-language movement. Our intention here is to provide data and interpretations useful to other educators in addressing by themselves the complex questions in these debates.

Language Resources

An increasing percentage of immigrant children have come from non-English-speaking countries during the past 100 years, and the public school system has been confronted with increasing difficulties because of the cultural diversity of immigrant students. Immigrant students pose a number of issues, some obvious and others less obvious, to the schools that serve them. The first and most obvious is language. The vast majority do not speak English. Teaching English to foreign students has always been a problem in U.S. schools, but strategies have been developed to cope with it (Montero-Sieburth & LaCelle-Peterson, 1991). Although the majority of immigrants in the past 100 years did not speak English when they first arrived, the task is becoming more complicated. Not only has the percentage of immigrants from non-English-speaking countries been increasing rapidly, but so has the variety of the languages the children bring with them. U.S. schools are now in a situation in which more than 100 languages are being spoken, and almost every language in the world has been spoken by some of its students.

Languages

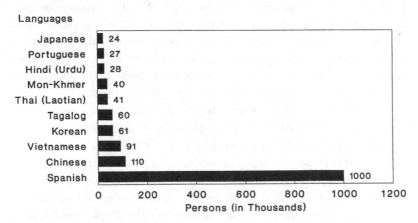

Figure 3.1. Top Ten Languages Other Than English Used by
Foreign-Born Children, U.S., 1990

SOURCE: U.S. Bureau of the Census (1993b).

Among the languages of the world, about 50 languages are spoken by
at least 10,000 of the students in the United States.

Figure 3.1 shows the top 10 languages that most foreign-born children were speaking in 1990. More than a million foreign-born children
spoke Spanish, and 110,000 children spoke Chinese. Vietnamese, Korean, Tagalog, Thai, Mon-Khmer, Hindi, Portuguese, and Japanese
were also common. Although half of the immigrant children who speak
a language other than English speak Spanish, many school systems
serve immigrant children who speak many different languages.

The design of language programs and the training and recruitment
of teachers and counselors in language services become more difficult
when taking into consideration the language variation within ethnic
and nationality groups. Although most Hispanic children in the United
States speak Spanish, some speak Portuguese and others use tongues
indigenous to areas of Latin America. Foreign-born children from Africa report speaking more than 50 different languages, and about 70
different languages are spoken by immigrant children who classified
themselves as Asians. Among the 70 languages, 25 are spoken by at
least 1,000 Asian immigrant children, and 11 languages are spoken by
at least 10,000 Asian immigrant children. Chinese immigrant children
alone speak 20 languages—for example, Thai, Malay, Vietnamese—although Chinese is the most common language spoken by more than

90% of Chinese foreign-born children. The linguistic situation becomes more complicated when considering different oral versions of certain languages. For example, the 110,000 foreign-born Chinese-speaking children are reportedly speaking eight different dialects. Speakers of Mandarin or Cantonese, the two most used dialects among Chinese Americans, cannot communicate with each other orally.

School districts need to know the number of languages spoken and the size of the populations who speak each of the languages to make long- and short-term plans for language and other services, allocating financial and human resources. School workshops that train teachers to speak a foreign language need to reflect differences among dialects to target teachers and map out an effective training plan. School districts hiring bilingual teachers must know whether the person they want to hire can speak the same dialect that their students speak. Of course, teachers are preferable who can speak not only various dialects of a language, but also several other languages.

Attrition and Retention
of Native Tongues

The data on immigrant adults indicate that about 80% of the newcomers speak a language other than English at home. More than 95% of Mexicans, Cubans, or Salvadorans spoke Spanish at home in 1990. About 90% of foreign-born people from the Philippines, Korea, Vietnam, or China also spoke their native languages at home, compared to 79% of those from Italy and 58% of those from Germany. Most non-English speakers who immigrate to the United States after they enter adulthood do not reach a high level of English proficiency and retain heavy foreign accents for the rest of their lives. The former Secretary of State, Henry Kissinger, who immigrated when he was nearly 18 years old, serves as a persuasive example. Linguistic cognition and language development for many immigrant adults are far beyond their control. Although language facility can always be improved, late language learners may never have the fluency of a native speaker. For this and other reasons, the language immigrant adults prefer to use at home is often their native tongues, especially if they have spouses who prefer and are able to speak the same language. More than half of those who spoke Spanish or an Asian or Pacific Islander language at home did not speak English "very well." In addition, 43% of the Mexican and nearly half of the Salvadoran foreign-born adults were *linguistically isolated,* a term used to designate those living in households in which no one who is 14 years old or older can speak English very well.

Several factors are related to child language retention and attrition: length of U.S. residency, age, gender, and family income. A child's race and ethnicity may also be an important factor. Race and ethnicity in the United States, probably everywhere in the world, are not necessarily biological. They may suggest a person's cultural heritage, language preference, religion, ethos, political beliefs, personal values, and, most important, a person's social and economic status. People are often viewed and treated differentially by their race and ethnicity according to the "social contract" or "status code" of racial stratification in the United States (Collins, 1988; Ogbu, 1982). These effects may compound problems associated with social class because many people in non-white groups have less education and lower income than the majority whites. We examine the consequences of each of these factors and their aggregated effects.

Among all foreign-born children, about 19% report speaking English at home. Most children of English-speaking homes came from countries or regions having English as a dominant or official language. Of all foreign-born children, 45% speak Spanish, 12% speak a non-English European language, and 23% of them speak an Asian language. Almost all children who reported a language other than English spoken at home also reported their ability to speak that language. Female children are slightly more likely to speak a non-English language than male children. Although higher-income families are likely to be English-only-speaking families, income makes no difference to a child's ability to speak a native tongue among the children whose family language is not English. Age has no relationship to native tongue speaking; children of various age groups are equally likely to speak a non-English language if their families do so. Hispanic children, by far, are the group most likely to speak a language other than English at home. For example, among foreign-born children who arrived in the United States between 1987 and 1990, 97% of Hispanic children, 95% of Asian children, and 79% of non-Hispanic white children (but only 38% of black children) reported speaking a language other than English. The longer children have resided in the United States, the less likely they are to speak their native tongues, although the native tongue's decline varies from group to group. Figure 3.2 shows a very slow decline of native tongue speaking for the total population; 90% of the newcomers who came

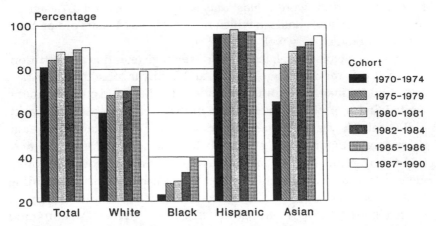

Figure 3.2. Foreign-Born Children Speaking a Language Other Than English at Home, U.S., 1990

SOURCE: U.S. Bureau of the Census (1993b).

between 1987 and 1990 were speaking a non-English native tongue, and 81% of immigrant youth who entered the United States between 1970 and 1975 were still speaking it after more than 15 years of residence. The decline of native language speaking is steeper for Asians (95% down to 65%) than for non-Hispanic whites (79% down to 60%). The length of residence, however, exerts no impact on native tongue speaking among Hispanic children: 96% of both the newest arrivals and the long-time U.S. residents spoke Spanish.

About 30% of all foreign-born children and over 40% of children who report non-English home languages were living in linguistically isolated households in 1990. Several factors contribute to the odds of living in a linguistically isolated home. First, family income level has a profound impact. Of children whose family income was lower than $15,000, 56% lived in a linguistically isolated household. Only 27% of children whose family income was higher than $30,000 lived in similar households. Among children who came to the United States between 1987 and 1990, Vietnamese children by far are the highest percentage (73%) living in a linguistically isolated home. More than half of Mexican (67%), other Hispanic (62%), and other Asian (51%) children also live in households linguistically isolated. In addition, 66% of children from Russia and other East European countries lived in a linguistically isolated household in 1990. Figure 3.3 shows that the longer children

reside in the United States, the less likely they are to live in a linguistically isolated household. Although 52% of all children who came to the
United States between 1987 and 1990 lived in a linguistically isolated
household in 1990, the percentage gradually declines to 36% for those who
came 5 years earlier and further drops to 18% for those who came to the
United States 10 years earlier. Finally, as revealed in Figure 3.4, younger
children are more likely to live in a linguistically isolated household
than older children when the year of entry is controlled. The percentage
of young children (5-9 years old) who lived in a linguistically isolated
household averages about 10% higher than for older children (15-17
years old). Although these data are for children who came to the United
States between 1987 and 1990, the pattern has been consistent among
other cohorts as well.

In summary, although native-tongue speaking declines for most
groups with the length of U.S. residence, use of the native tongue by
children whose home languages are not English persists. Although
many groups have continued to speak their native tongues after arriving, most have quickly broken the household linguistic isolation.
Among the children who came to the United States between 1975 and
1979, 96% of Mexican children still speak Spanish at home, but the percentage of Mexican children who still live in a linguistically isolated
household has decreased from 67% among the newest arrivals (between 1987 and 1990) to 24% for those who have lived in the United
States 15 years or longer. The census data present many similar contrasts. Of Vietnamese children, 94% still speak their native tongues after
15 years of residence in the United States, but the linguistic isolation of
household has been cut two thirds from 73% for the newest arrivals to
23% for people who have lived here more than 15 years. Of Russian,
Eastern European, and Middle Eastern immigrants, 9 of 10 still speak
their native tongues after 15 or more years of residence in the United
States, 8 of 9 of these families having broken the linguistic isolation, up
from 1 of 3 for recent Russian and Eastern European immigrants and 1
of 2 for Middle Eastern immigrants.

Recognition of all the links of linguistic adaptation is important for
facilitating immigrant children's language transition. Acquiring standard English has been a crucial prerequisite for immigrants to make a
successful adjustment to the new society. On the other hand, mastery of
the new language is not simply a matter of learning a new technical
skill. Especially if acquisition of the new language is seen as the first
step in losing the native tongue, achievement of mastery over the

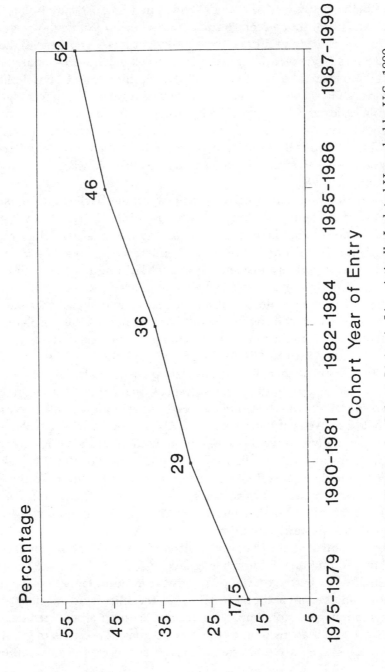

Figure 3.3. Foreign-Born Children, by Cohort, Living in Linguistically Isolated Households, U.S., 1990
SOURCE: U.S. Bureau of the Census (1993b).

42

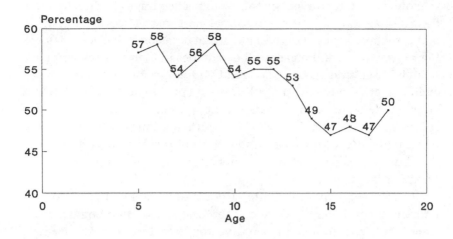

Figure 3.4. Foreign-Born Children of the 1987-1990 Cohort Living in Linguistically Isolated Households by Age, U.S., 1990

SOURCE: U.S. Bureau of the Census (1993b).

language of a receiving society may be a profound psychological and sociological event to immigrant children and their families. It may even be seen as the first step in rejecting the original homeland and may consequently be resisted, consciously or unconsciously, by immigrants themselves or, in the case of children, by their parents (cf. Rodriguez, 1982). A very practical educational issue is also involved. Pain and frustration occur within immigrant families because of the loss of effective communication between native-speaker parents and English-only-speaking children. Children need parental guidance and direction during their growth. Immigrant children who acculturate into a society unfamiliar and alienated at best, hostile and rejecting at worst, may need more help and comfort from their parents than do native-born children. Conversations on intimate topics, such as friendship, dating, and marriage, are difficult enough without attempting them across language barriers.

Many linguists and developmental psychologists have argued that the ability to speak a native tongue may help a child learn English better, and many experienced teachers, social workers, and sociologists agree that open communication between children and parents helps the child profoundly in many ways that directly or indirectly relate to schooling and later career. Schools need to encourage children to retain their mother tongues—if not in formal class instruction, then in informal activities, such as cultural and social occasions. Teachers may ask their immigrant children about the activities in their Sunday language schools—weekend classes provided by immigrant volunteers to teach children native language and culture—and praise children for this extra effort made to retain their native tongues. Foreign language speech competitions are useful activities encouraging immigrant students to be bilingual. Unfortunately, competitions of this kind usually involve only European languages such as French and Spanish, rarely any Asian or Arabic languages.

In our own experience, after 10 or more years of U.S. residency, immigrant children fully develop their oral and written English proficiency but tend to lose their native tongues. In that case, teachers should assess the whole family's linguistic situation, including the family's language background, the parents' English proficiency, and parental education, to make recommendations to their students. At the least, teachers can ask their students how they can communicate with their non-English-speaking parents if they decide to give up their native tongue completely, a question we have asked our own linguistic minority students many times. Schools should not see a child's speaking a language other than English as a hindrance to the child's improvement of his or her English. Historically, efforts advocated in U.S. schools for English acquisition have ignored invisible endeavors for native language retention and the sorrow for native language attrition of immigrant children and their families. U.S. schools cannot effectively teach every immigrant child English unless all links of linguistic adaptation are addressed. We urge greater modeling of language learning among Europeans, Asian Indians, and other settings where multilingual communities are the norm rather than the exception.

English Acquisition

One of the principal indicators of accommodation to a new culture is the ability to communicate effectively in the common language. Martin and Midgley (1994) report that at the end of the 20th century, as it was at the century's beginning, most immigrants arrive not speaking English. In the 1990 census, 32 million people reported that they spoke a language other than English at home, and 14 million of them said they did not "speak English very well." About 48% of the 17.3 million U.S. residents whose home language was Spanish did not speak English "very well," and the 4.5 million who spoke an Asian or Pacific language at home had still greater difficulty: 54% reported not speaking English "very well." Barring a new priority for language teaching and learning, at current rates of immigration these numbers cannot be expected to decline; as soon as immigrants and their children learn English, they are replaced in the pool of non-English speakers by new immigrants.

Linguistic adaptation refers to a situation wherein a person speaks two languages simultaneously and switches smoothly back and forth between languages. To cope with this complicated situation, many linguistic, psychological, and social skills have to be learned initially, especially for those whose languages are so different from English—such as Chinese, Vietnamese, Arabic, and many African languages. With few exceptions, newcomers unable to speak English in the Anglo-American world face enormous obstacles. Learning English is a basic step to enable new immigrants to participate in the life of the larger community, get an education, find a job, obtain access to health care or social services, and apply for citizenship. Language has often been cited as the principal initial barrier confronting recent immigrants, from the least educated farm workers to the most educated professionals. According to Portes and Rumbaut (1996), educators need to be sure the process of language learning—played out, particularly for the children of new immigrants, in the institutional context of the public schools—is a mutual adaptation, an accommodation of multiple ethnolinguistic groups in particular structural contexts.

The U.S. Bureau of the Census inquired about a person's ability to speak English in the 1990 census. People who filled out the census long-form questionnaire were asked to evaluate themselves and others in the household for oral English usage using the following categories:

- Very well—no difficulty in speaking English, the level considered as oral English proficiency
- Well—minor to moderate problems
- Not well—seriously limited
- Not at all—spoke no English at all

Scholars (e.g., Heath, 1986; Jiobu, 1988) have argued that many factors are involved in English acquisition: place of birth, length of time in the United States, social class and parental education, family language, neighborhood language diversity and English environment, availability of schooling, and quality of ESL or bilingual education program. They believe that a child's progress in English learning is a product of the combination of all those effects.

According to census data, among the 2.2 million foreign-born children, 5.5% (120,000) reported speaking no English, 13.2% (about 300,000) reported speaking very limited English, and 22% (about 500,000) reported minor or moderate problems in speaking English. Altogether, about one million children, 40% of all foreign-born children, had difficulty speaking English. Furthermore, some percentage of foreign-born children, especially immigrant children in middle and high school, who reported speaking English very well, might still have severe problems in reading and writing English. Learning subject matter at these grade levels requires a much higher level of English mastery than simply speaking it.

According to Stevens (1992), although many factors are involved, foreign-born children who grow up in families where English is the only spoken language learn English more easily than children raised in homes where a language other than English is spoken. For the majority of immigrant children, however, the home language as well as other home elements are givens, not choices. Their English learning is affected by these givens.

Why do some children—as well as some adults—learn English quicker, better, and more easily than others? A hidden factor here may be English exposure before immigration. English has become the worldwide language of business, science and technology, and youth cultures. With the exception of very young children, immigrants arrive in the United States with an existing linguistic repertoire. The linguistic attributes of newcomers are the product of language-specific selection processes (Stevens, 1994). First, all other things being equal, potential immigrants, born and raised in countries in which English is a dominant or official language, have a large advantage over potential immigrants born and raised in non-English language countries. A considerable proportion of the immigrants legally admitted to the United States during the 1970s and 1980s had some exposure to English before migrating. About a quarter of the immigrants legally admitted during the 1970s and 1980s were from English language countries. Second, people who did not come from English language countries believed that expo-

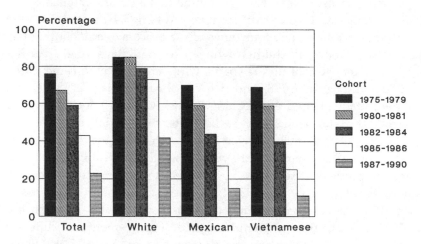

Figure 3.5. Foreign-Born Children Speaking English Very Well by Cohort, U.S., 1990

SOURCE: U.S. Bureau of the Census (1993b).

sure to English through education, training, and social and cultural life in home countries was important to the rapidity and ease with which they adjusted to an English-language-dominated environment. Although the linguistic characteristics of immigrants on arriving in the United States contribute to their children's acquisition of English, these data are generally unavailable.

All theories of second-language learning acknowledge the role of time. Over time and with increased exposure to second-language input, individuals' levels of proficiency in a second language increase. Figure 3.5 shows the distributions of immigrants' self-reported speaking proficiency in English in 1990 across selected race and ethnic groups by the year of immigration. The data presented in Figure 3.5 show that oral English proficiency increases across the immigrant children's entry cohorts for all groups and thus presumably increases with the time lived in the United States. This general finding—and the interpretation that this relationship reflects English language acquisition as it occurs in the United States—is common (Jasso & Rosenzweig, 1990). Length of residence in the United States is probably the best single measure, however crude, of amount of exposure to English language input.

Figure 3.5 also reveals race and ethnic effects on oral English acquisition. Groups starting with different levels of English mastery improve at different paces, and the outcomes of the process over a period of 15 years vary. Among all children who spoke a language other than English at home, 40% of non-Hispanic white children who came to the United States between 1987 and 1990 can speak English very well, and the percentage of children speaking English very well nearly doubled among those who came 2 years earlier. After the 5 initial years, the pace for language adjustment slowed down somewhat for non-Hispanic whites, and after a period of 10 years the rates for oral English proficiency improvement settled at about 80%. A similar pattern occurred among the earlier cohort of 1970-1974. The various cohorts of Vietnamese followed a pattern resembling the non-Hispanic white children, but with different beginning points and with improvement at a different pace. Only one in 10 Vietnamese children who came to the United States between 1987 and 1990 reported oral English proficiency—representing the lowest level of any group. The percentage of children reporting oral English proficiency doubled every 3 years, however, and after 10 to 15 years of U.S. residence, three quarters of Vietnamese immigrant children reportedly spoke English very well. No reported significant further improvement in oral English can be traced back, however, to the earlier cohort of 1970-1974. Mexican immigrant children showed a pattern very similar to the Vietnamese children.

Table 3.1 presents the percentage of children in various cohorts who came from non-English language families in 1990, but who reported oral English proficiency. This table reports the oral English proficiency for total foreign-born children and for seven selected groups. We incorporate family income into our inquiry to examine socioeconomic impact on immigrant children's linguistic transition and acculturation to U.S. society.

Immigrant children from families with higher incomes are more likely to have oral English proficiency than those from lower-income families. Census data reveal a substantial gap in oral English proficiency between middle-class immigrant children and the poor. Among all foreign-born children who spoke a language other than English at home, 56% who came from families with an income of $30,000 or higher, reported a command of oral English compared to 45% who came from families with an income between $15,000 to $30,000, and 40% who came from families with an income below $15,000. The size of the gap between the more or less affluent groups varies across time and

TABLE 3.1 Foreign-Born Children[a] (aged 5-18) Who Reported
Speaking English Very Well for Selected Race/Ethnic
Groups,[b] Year of Entry,[c] and Family Income,[d] U.S., 1990
(in percentages)

	1975-1979	1980-1981	1982-1984	1985-1986	1987-1990
Total					
Low	69	62	50	35	19
High	80	73	68	51	29
Whites					
Low	78	79	69	59	29
High	88	87	81	79	52
Caribbean Blacks					
Low	88	61	63	43	37
High	89	72	63	51	33
African Blacks					
Low	69	81	65	52	42
High	79	73[e]	71	57	46
Mexicans					
Low	65	57	42	28	13
High	73	62	44	25	14
Other Hispanics					
Low	79	71	61	40	19
High	84	81	73	52	24
Asians					
Low	78	63	58	44	21
High	82	78	75	62	34
Southeast Asians					
Low	63	57	38	28	11
High	78	63	46	32	15

NOTE: Data from U.S. Bureau of the Census (1993b).
a. Only children who reported speaking a language other than English at
home included.
b. Whites includes only non-Hispanic whites who came from countries
where English was not the dominant language. Caribbean blacks include
Haitians and Jamaicans. African blacks include blacks from any country on
the African continent. Other Hispanics include all people who classified
themselves as Hispanic, except Mexicans, and Puerto Ricans who are not
immigrants. Asians include all Asians except Southeast Asians. Southeast
Asians include Cambodians, Laotians, Hmong, and Vietnamese.
c. Year of entry = the year immigrants entered the United States.
d. Family income = low was $15,000 or less in 1990; high was $30,000 or
more in 1990. To simplify the table, we omitted the people whose family
income was between $15,000 and $30,000.
e. The number of children in this cell is too small to obtain reliable
information.

racial and ethnic groups. Family income contributes heavily to oral English proficiency in the first 3 to 5 years of children's immigration, but this impact gradually diminishes as the length of U.S. residence increases. For all children who immigrated to the United States between 1987 and 1990, those from higher-income families were 53% more likely to have oral English proficiency than their counterparts with less affluent backgrounds. The size of the gap gradually reduced with each cohort. Among the 1975-1979 cohort, children from higher-income families are only 16% more likely to have oral English proficiency than their less affluent counterparts.

If the pace of improvement in oral English proficiency serves as one of the indicators of acculturation to U.S. society, non-Hispanic white children have steadily adapted. Caribbean black children and African black children also seem more acculturated than the other groups, at least during the first 3 years after immigration. Non-Hispanic white children from higher-income families are more likely to speak English very well than other children in each of the five cohorts, and white children from lower-income families are also more likely to have oral English proficiency than other children from the same economic background in each of the five cohorts, except African blacks in the 1980-1981 cohort and Caribbean blacks in the 1975-1979 cohort. The reliability of that information is, however, questionable because of the small number of children in those two cells. The effect of family income on English proficiency is greater for groups with more socioeconomic disparity than for the groups concentrated on one end of the income scale. The impact of family income on English proficiency is less impressive and even reversed among Southeast Asians, Mexicans, and Caribbean and African blacks who are more concentrated at the lower end of the income scale. Our other data sources indicate the gap is also less apparent for the Japanese, who are concentrated at the higher end of the income scale.

Age is another influence on children's English acquisition. The curve in Figure 3.6 reveals that both younger and older children may be more vulnerable in linguistic adaptation. Of young children who had resided in the United States 3 or less years, 20% reportedly could not speak any English in 1990. The percentage declined with the increase in children's age, although it rose again dramatically among children 15 years or older. A quarter of 18-year-olds spoke no English at all.

Although male children were more likely in 1990 to report that they came from families where English is the primary language, among the

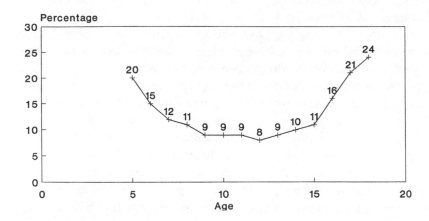

Figure 3.6. Foreign-Born Children of the 1987-1990 Cohort Speaking No English by Age, U.S., 1990

SOURCE: U.S. Bureau of the Census (1993b).

children who spoke a language other than English at home, females were slightly more likely than males to reach oral English proficiency. Males were also more likely than females to report speaking no English at all (15% male vs. 7% female). Otherwise, patterns of variation in oral English proficiency were not significantly different by sex.

Furthermore, linguistic theories (e.g., Stevens, 1994) imply that individuals with less education are disadvantaged in the acquisition of a complex cognitive skill such as proficiency in a second language. Data from other sources indicate that among lesser-educated young adolescents who immigrated as school-aged children, lack of literacy in their first language is an impediment to second-language learning.

To summarize the language patterns we have presented, younger children, children recently immigrated, those from lower-socioeconomic families, those who live in the inner city, and those who are members of certain ethnic groups are apparently disadvantaged in developing oral English proficiency when compared to other children, and the aggregated effects of all these factors may significantly hinder immigrant children's chances to improve their English. This is especially true for very young children and adolescents.

The census data we have compiled indicate that seven of ten 5-year-old children have difficulties speaking English. Among them, a third cannot speak any English at all. Migration during this critical period of language development can devastate children not only in their linguistic skills in a first language, but also in concept development, logical reasoning, and other cognitive abilities. Many researchers have suggested that children lacking age-appropriate skills in their first language have added difficulties when trying to learn a second language. That may be the case for many young immigrant learners with limited English. Our findings also indicate that young children are more likely to live in a linguistically isolated household (see Figure 3.4) than older children, and they are also more likely to be from families with lower incomes who reside in inner cities. Because of language barriers, lack of information and networks, or long working hours from holding two or three jobs, parents may not know where and how to find help for their children. A much higher percentage of 5- to 7-year-old immigrant children have not attended school than native children. For example, among 6-year-old children, 12% of foreign-born children were not enrolled in school compared to 7% of native-born children; among the 7-year-olds, the ratio is 7.4% versus 5%. Absence from schools may initially result from the lack of oral English proficiency among these young children, but it further aggravates the English acquisition problem. Head Start programs designed to help children from disadvantaged backgrounds must make every effort to reach out to these immigrant children and to recruit them actively into their programs. In the following chapter we focus on the educational achievement of immigrant children.

4

Educational
Attainment

The rapid expansion of the population of immigrant children-of-color in U.S. schools has caused educators and policymakers to review knowledge and information on these children's educational performance and to reexamine the policies for these children's schooling. Students of Asian and Hispanic origin comprise the largest proportions of recent immigrant students—having increased 158% and 68%, respectively, in U.S. elementary and secondary schools from 1976 to 1990. The numbers of immigrants from the Caribbean and Africa have also increased steadily and considerably.

In this chapter, we discuss the patterns and levels of educational attainment of immigrant children and examine the relationship between these children's schooling and other demographic and socioeconomic factors, including their language transition. The first section of this chapter addresses the educational attainment of immigrant children compared to native children. The second section examines the variability of educational attainment between and within ethnic and nationality groups.

We use three categories of indicators: (a) general educational enrollment; (b) educational progression, including educational acceleration, retention, and detainment; and (c) rates for school completion at elementary, middle, and high school levels, with a focus on the high school dropout problem. These measures are analyzed across racial groups, ethnic groups, nationality groups, age, gender, year of immigration, socioeconomic status, and other relevant factors. In the third section of this chapter, we examine how immigrant children's educational attainment relates to their linguistic adaptation in the United States and what that means to educators. This material demonstrates that immigrant students cannot be viewed as a single group: Relevant comparisons must be made across immigrants from different ethnic and nationality groups, and between immigrants and native-born individuals in general and of the same ethnic and nationality groups.

For measures of educational progression, we use two classifications: "under-age" (acceleration) and "over-age" (detainment). Census data do not provide information on enrollment at specific grade levels. We therefore use general enrollment information and grade completion data to assess children's progress in school. The grade that the highest percentage of children completed at a certain age provides a measure of average grade level for each age group—it is referred to as the age-adjusted grade. Children of a given age who are enrolled in school and indicate completion of a specific grade above or below the average level for the age group are classified as under-age or over-age.

The Educational Attainment
of Foreign-Born and Native-Born Children

People often believe that immigrants do not do as well as native-born students because they are disadvantaged by immigration to and settlement in the new country. Besides the generally lower economic and educational status of immigrant parents, researchers (Verdonk, 1982) have considered other disadvantages that immigrant children may have.

1. English is not the primary language and is not effectively used in the home.
2. Immigrant children may not get enough support from families because parents may not speak English well or even understand the U.S. educational system. Contacts between parents and schools are negligible.
3. Ideas and norms immigrant parents have about schooling and raising children may conflict with those espoused in schools.

4. Many immigrants and their families suffer from uncertain legal status. Alienated in this way, children from these families may not be socialized as well as native children.
5. A gap occurs between institutional integration, which is access to government-subsidized or -created institutions, and social integration, which is access to interpersonal contacts. Discrimination is forbidden by law, but occurs in fact.

This characterization, however, represents only some immigrants. Educational historians have established that a disproportionate share of the best educated and most successful adults and of the children performing best in school are immigrants or the first-generation children of immigrants. The German children who did well in the 19th century and the Jewish children who achieved educational success in the early 20th century (Ravitch, 1974) received little attention from the public (cf. Glazer, 1977). Reports in the newspapers focused on the anxiety, complaints, and panicked cries from city educational bureaus and community educational boards about shortages of teachers, lack of school buildings, and poor teaching facilities. In recent years, young Cubans have completed more years of education than non-Hispanic whites (U.S. Bureau of the Census, 1983b), and the academic accomplishment of Asian American children has attracted attention from researchers, news media, and the public (Hirschman & Wong, 1986; Suzuki, 1977; Wei, 1986). International studies reveal that immigrant minorities have done well in many parts of the world: Greeks, Yugoslavs, and Italians in Australia (Taft & Cahill, 1981); and many language minority immigrants in Canada (Anisef, 1975).

Many current studies contradict conventional beliefs. Gibson (1988) has claimed mounting evidence that immigrant youth do comparatively well in school, especially if they receive most of their education in their new homeland. Immigrants, on the whole, have higher educational and occupational aspirations than indigenous groups, majority as well as minority, and are more determined than nonimmigrants of comparable class background to use education as a strategy for upward social mobility. Immigrant parents and children assume that education can enhance opportunities to compete for jobs. High expectations and assumptions about the value of schooling appear to have far more impact on the immigrant child's decision to persist in school than either family background or actual school performance.

Many teachers who have had immigrant students share this optimistic view. McDonnell and Hill (1993) report that teachers who worked with immigrant children found the experience to be uncommonly rewarding. These teachers believed that recently immigrated students were better motivated and "brighter" than their native-born or more established immigrant students. Los Angeles transcript data also show that immigrant elementary school students have better attendance records than their U.S.-born or more established immigrant classmates. These patterns do not, however, persist long after immigration. As some teachers have told us, immigrant students Americanize all too soon. But during their first few years in the United States, they are especially rewarding pupils. Unfortunately, census data do not measure educational aspirations or other psychosocial factors, despite their relationship to children's schooling.

Until recently, the education of immigrants lagged behind that of natives. In her dissertation, Rong (1988) shows that for a century foreign-born whites who came to the United States have had far less education than native whites, and their foreign-born children have done less well than native-born white children in U.S. schools. She also reports that the gap in enrollment rates between foreign-born white children and native white children has narrowed over the years: from a ratio of 2:3 in 1890 to almost no difference in 1970. The narrowed gap may reflect the progress during the past half century in spreading educational opportunity into the South and other rural areas. The U.S. public school system has opened itself to more classes and races than ever before.

Our study shows, however, that the gap between the foreign born and native born remains. Foreign-born children as a whole, regardless of race and ethnicity, had lower school enrollment rates than native white children. In 1990, for all groups, 93% of 6- to 16-year-old foreign-born children were enrolled in schools, compared to 94.5% of native-born children. Figure 4.1 shows, however, that the largest gap in enrollment rates between these two groups occurs at the two ends of the age cohorts. Actually, both foreign-born and native-born children who are very young (aged 5-7 years) or who are older (15+ years) are more likely to be absent from school than children in other age cohorts. This pattern may partly be due to the problems of linguistic transition and linguistic environments for very young children and adolescents that we discuss in Chapter 3. It also suggests the age groups needing attention, resources, and energy to correct this schooling problem.

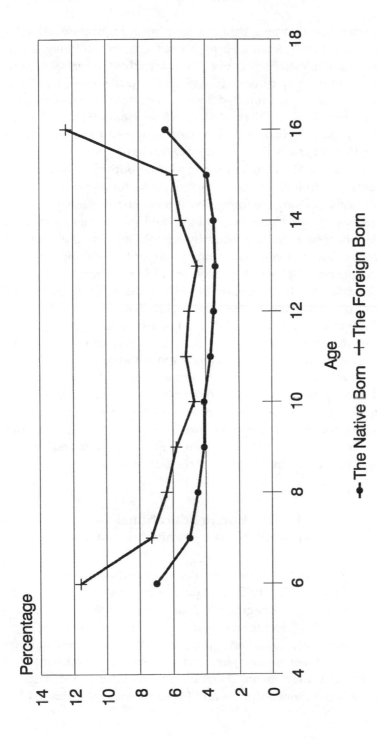

Figure 4.1. Children Aged 6-16 Reportedly Not in Schools by Nativity and Age, U.S., 1990
SOURCE: U.S. Bureau of the Census (1993b).

As a whole, foreign-born children have lower high school completion rates. For example, among 12- to 18-year-olds, 95% of foreign-born
children had completed 5 years of elementary education in 1990 compared to 96% of the native born. Among the 14- to 18-year-olds, 68% of
foreign-born children had finished 8 years of middle school compared
to 75% of native-born children. Among 18-year-olds, 31% of foreign
born had finished 12 years of high school compared to 43% of native
born. The dropout rate is much higher for foreign-born youth than for
native-born youth: About 26% of foreign-born youth drop out of high
school compared to 11% of natives. Illiteracy rates for dropout youth are
also much higher among the foreign born than among the native born.
Because of language problems, frequent local and long-distance migration
of families, inappropriate placements by schools, and starting school at
later ages, foreign-born youth take much longer to finish high school
than do native born: 31% of 18- to 20-year-old foreign-born youth were
still in high school in 1990 compared to 18% of the native born.

Educational attainment varies, however, because of many factors
across these ethnic and nationality groups. Many immigrant groups
perform better academically than native-born children in general, although they may not do better than their native-born peers from similar
ethnic and nationality groups. A few groups among the foreign-born
population do perform equally to or surpass such native-born peers.
Grant and Rong (1996) have reported that immigrant white male youth
aged 15-24 years who were from English-language-speaking countries
completed more years of schooling than their U.S.-born peers. This diversity and variability are the focus of the next section.

The Variation in Educational
Attainment of Immigrant Children

Immigrants in the 1990s are the most diverse population ever to come
to the United States. They bring a variety of experiences and skills as
well as diverse cultural backgrounds. Many arrive with education and
job skills and quickly become economic contributors as scientists, engineers, professors, artists, and entrepreneurs. Other immigrants, however, encounter numerous problems and barriers to successful integration into the U.S. mainstream. For example, one third of immigrant
workers are high school dropouts and therefore may have limited En-

glish skills, or may be illiterate in their own languages. Refugees may have suffered psychologically and physically in labor camps and jails before leaving their home countries. These divergent backgrounds are reflected in patterns of settlement in the United States and may affect children's linguistic transition and education in schools. This diversity requires flexibility from state and local policymakers to help newcomers become self-sufficient learners in schools.

Contrary to evidence from previous research, we show that the amount of education an immigrant student may have in the United States varies widely depending on race and ethnicity, nation of origin, age and gender, socioeconomic status, and year of entry and length of residence. In Chapter 2, we have reported patterns of education for incoming immigrants that are oddly bipolar compared to the native-born population: Foreign-born adults are both more likely than the native born to have less than a high school education and more likely to have graduated from college and gotten a degree from graduate or professional schools. We discuss several emergent questions on attainment in this section, such as dichotomous performances across groups, effects of immigration waves on performance, and age effects. In evaluating these data, we stress that average levels of education of certain immigrant groups vary over time.

Enrollment

Of all 6- to 16-year-old foreign-born children, 93% were enrolled in schools in 1990—86% in public schools and 7% in private schools. Total enrollment rates vary little across groups: 97% of non-Hispanic whites who came from English-speaking countries, followed by 96% of Asian children, 95% of Southeast Asian children, 94% of black children from Africa and non-Hispanic whites who came from non-English-speaking countries, and 93% of Caribbean black children and Hispanic non-Mexican children. Mexican immigrant children have the lowest enrollment rates: Only 88% of Mexican children were in school in 1990. White children were more likely to be in private schools than other children: 18% of the non-Hispanic white children who came from English-speaking countries and 16% of non-Hispanic whites who came from non-English-speaking countries were enrolled in private schools, compared to 2% of Mexican and Southeast Asian children. The range for other groups' private school enrollment rates is 5%-7%, much lower than that of white children.

Educational Progression

Educational progression is the pace at which children move through levels of schooling. This is affected by other measures, such as school starting age, dropout rates, and detention at one or two grades. Children who start school early and persist through each year's academic agenda are ahead of other children. Immigrant children often start school later than native children and are more likely to become dropouts than native-born children. Rong (1988), however, reports, using U.S. census data from 1950 and 1970, that although foreign-born white children had higher rates of lagging behind their age-adjusted grade level in school (over-age), a relatively high percentage in this group were also ahead of their age-adjusted grade level (under-age), another of the bipolar patterns common to immigrants in the aggregate. Among all ethnic or nationality groups, Japanese children had the highest school enrollment rates at ages 5-18 and the highest enrollment rates and lowest over-age rates for ages 6-16. Chinese children are the group most likely to seek higher education, especially postbaccalaureate studies, and they constitute the highest percentage of under-age 5- to 18-year-olds, being ahead of their age-adjusted grade level, among all race and ethnic groups.

Our 1990 census data reveal that African immigrant children had the highest age-adjusted completion rates at various levels of schooling. By the age of 10, 30% of black immigrant children from Africa had completed 5 years of elementary school, compared to an average completion rate of 26% for all foreign-born children at that age. By age 13, black immigrant children from Africa and the Caribbean had a 7.5% 8-year middle school completion rate, also the highest among all foreign-born groups. At age 16, 6% of black immigrant youths from Africa and the Caribbean had graduated from high school, compared to a 2.6% average graduation rate for all foreign-born youth at that age level.

Schooling Completion

Using available census data, we have found an inconsistent effect of year of entry cohorts on school completion at various levels of education; furthermore, no significant gender difference occurs at any of the three levels of schooling—elementary, middle school, or high school. Although dropout rates are higher for male immigrants than for female immigrants, this pattern is consistent for all groups in U.S. society.

Of course, age does affect children's educational attainment; therefore, attainment data are reported with age specification wherever possible.

Of all foreign-born children between the ages of 12 and 18, 95% had completed 5 years of elementary school in 1990, including all the white children from English language countries and 93.3% of Mexican children. No wide range of variations in this percentage occurs among the ethnic and nationality groups for the cohorts of different entry years or between males and females. Of foreign-born teenagers between the ages of 14 and 18, 68% had finished 8-year middle school, including 80% of white teenagers from English language countries and 63% of Mexican immigrant children. The range for the percentage of middle school completion among other groups runs from 71% among other Hispanic teens to 79% among Asian teens. The largest disparity in attainment is the high school graduate rates. At age 18, 32% of immigrant youths had graduated from high school. This is significantly lower than the percentage of native-born children who graduated. White youths from English language countries were, however, almost four times more likely than Mexican youths to have graduated from high school by age 18 (66.4% vs. 18%). With high school graduation rates of 26% at age 18, youth from other Hispanic groups and Southeast Asia were the next groups that compared unfavorably to whites from non-English language countries (50%), black children from Africa (45%), Asian children (44%), and Caribbean black children (40%).

We have mentioned before that the lower completion rates for several language minority groups can be attributed to many personal and instrumental factors. Some people, of all ages, foreign born and native, have never been in any school. The majority of people neither in school nor holding a high school diploma have, however, dropped out of school, most from high school. Although each state sets different legal ages for youths to leave school, all states require school attendance until age 16. We believe the school dropout issue is central to the educational attainment problems of youths of many ethnic and nationality groups, especially among Hispanic groups—Mexican, Dominican, and Central American immigrant youth. Because measuring school dropout rates involves assessment of enrollment, school progression, and school completion, we discuss the problem in a separate section.

School Dropout

We have used several census questions to explore the school drop-out problem. The criterion is a person aged 12 to 18, who self-reportedly had not completed 12 years of school, and who was not in school when the census long-form was completed. The majority of these people left after a few years of high school, although 13% never reached that stage, and 3% never started middle school. Table 4.1 shows the school drop-out rates by ethnicity and nationality, age, and dropout status. In 1990, among all native-born 17-year-olds, the dropout rate was 9%; among 18-year-olds it was 13%. Of the 17-year-old foreign born, however, 18% were dropouts, and this grew to 26% for those aged 18. White youth from English language countries and youths of both Asian groups had lower dropout rates than the average for the total native-born youth in the same age range. The rates for whites from non-English language countries, African blacks, and Caribbean black youths were not signifi-cantly different from the native born. The two Hispanic groups, espe-cially the Mexican youths, however, had significantly higher dropout rates than the native born. At age 17, 34% of Mexican immigrants who had not graduated from high school were not in school, and the per-centage increased to 48% at age 18. Of Mexican youths, 4% of 17-year-olds and 6% of 18-year-olds did not even finish 5 years of elementary school. Mexican youths account for one third of the 17- to 18-year-old foreign-born population, but two thirds of the dropouts in that group. Among the 90,000 immigrant youths aged 17 to 18 who were dropouts in the United States, 60,000 of them were Mexicans, including 7,000 Mexican youth with less than 5 years of schooling.

Fourteen is the crucial age when foreign-born youth begin to leave school in large numbers without a high school diploma (see Figure 4.2). This varies, however, from group to group: Mexican youth begin leav-ing school at much younger ages; by 14 the dropout rate for Mexican children is already radically different from other groups. The gap, how-ever, in educational attainment between Mexicans and other groups for those under 14 years old is smaller compared to the one after that criti-cal age. Given that foreign-born Mexican children also have late school entry, we speculate that a large percentage of the Mexican youth who were dropouts may never have entered high school. In contrast, the beginning point for dropout behaviors among the total foreign-born population is age 16, 2 years older than that for Mexican youth. For total native-born youth and Asian youth, the beginning for dropping out is after age 16—the legal age for most states (see Figure 4.2).

TABLE 4.1 School Dropouts by Ethnic-Nationality Group and Education Level, U.S., 1990

	Age	Non-High School Dropouts[a] (in percentages)	Dropouts (in percentages) < 5 Years	≥ 5 Years
Total native born	17	90.6	0.2	9.2
	18	87.5	0.3	12.2
Total foreign born	17	82.0	1.7	16.3
	18	74.3	2.7	23.0
White[b]	17	94.8	0.0	5.2
	18	95.3	0.0	4.7
White[c]	17	91.0	0.4	8.6
	18	89.0	1.0	10.0
Black Caribbean	17	90.7	0.4	8.9
	18	89.0	0.0	11.0
African Black	17	90.2	0.6	9.2
	18	89.2	1.3	9.5
Mexican	17	65.5	3.9	30.6
	18	51.8	5.5	42.7
Other Hispanic	17	83.5	1.5	15.0
	18	74.0	2.6	23.4
Asian	17	95.5	0.1	4.4
	18	95.2	0.2	4.6
Southeast Asian	17	93.8	0.5	5.7
	18	92.3	0.7	7.0

NOTE: Data from U.S. Bureau of the Census (1993b). Caribbean blacks include Haitians and Jamaicans. African blacks include blacks from any country on the African continent. Other Hispanics include all people who classified themselves as Hispanic, except Mexicans, and Puerto Ricans who are not immigrants. Asians include all Asians except Southeast Asians. Southeast Asians include Cambodians, Laotians, Hmong, and Vietnamese.
a. Non-high school dropouts indicate persons who either graduated from high school or still were in school.
b. Includes only non-Hispanic whites who came from countries where English was the dominant and official language.
c. Includes only non-Hispanic whites who came from countries where English was not the dominant language.

Length of residence in the United States decreases the dropout rate among the foreign born. Figure 4.3 shows a two-thirds reduction in the dropout rates among 18-year-olds and a three-quarters reduction

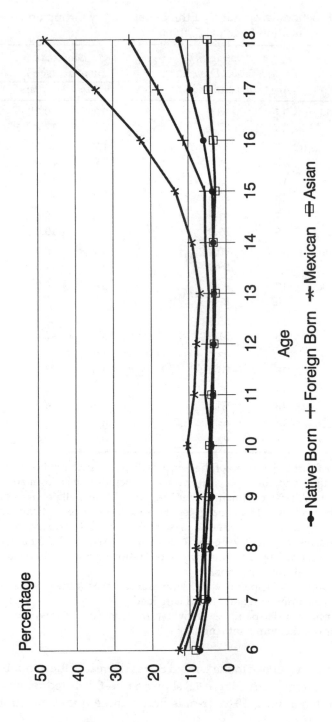

Figure 4.2. Children Aged 6-18 Neither in School Nor High School Graduates for Selected Groups, U.S., 1990
SOURCE: U.S. Bureau of the Census (1993b).

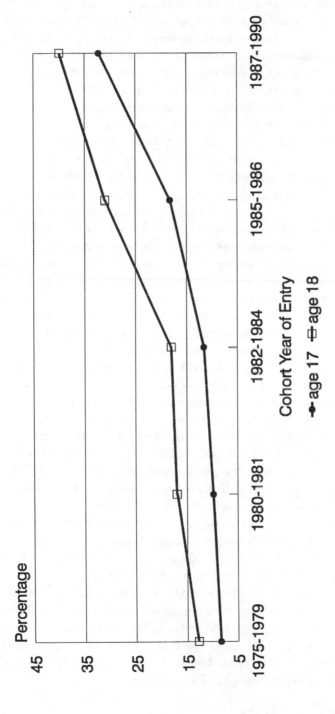

Figure 4.3. Foreign Born Neither in School Nor High School Graduates by Age and Cohort, U.S., 1990
SOURCE: U.S. Bureau of the Census (1993b).

among 17-year-olds for cohorts who came to this country between 1975-1979 compared to cohorts who came during 1987-1990. Figure 4.4 further elaborates the trend and presents two diverse versions. Among the newest Mexican 17-year-old comers, the dropout rate was 57%. It declined considerably, however, among the cohort residing in the United States for 10 to 15 years, whose dropout rates were only slightly higher than the native born. This trend also occurs among Southeast Asian youth. The pattern of dropping out among cohorts of black youth from Africa is inconsistent with the general pattern, perhaps partially explained by the extremely small number of black immigrants in the United States in the earlier cohort, or by the different ethnic groups who formed the majority of various immigrant waves from Africa.

Dropping out of school is a very serious problem among the foreign-born population. Immigrant youth who do not complete middle school or even elementary school join those consigned to illiteracy or semiliteracy. They face difficulty in promoting themselves occupationally, and they may even be unable to manage basic functions in this technological and service-oriented society. Most alarming is the uneven distribution of illiteracy and semiliteracy across ethnic and nationality groups. This pattern threatens U.S. democratic principles of equality, equity, social mobility, and political stability.

The causes of illiteracy and dropping out of school among immigrant youth are multifarious, but not mysterious. Many immigrant students, especially the most recent ones and those with no psychological, academic, and linguistic preparation before immigration, have difficulty functioning in U.S. classrooms. Most take several years to gain a working knowledge of English, and the secondary school curriculum demands both language competence and interpersonal skills. Students who have made progress in their home-country schools can usually take regular mathematics courses within the first year of immigrating because math relies less on English facility and because the mathematics curricula in many foreign countries is more demanding than in the United States. Nevertheless, students whose education has been disrupted by immigration often take much longer to catch up in secondary school. Therefore, the transition they make may be too slow. Before they have a chance to catch up, they are already older than their classmates. Few teenage immigrants who enter U.S. schools with deficient academic preparation ever make the transition to full-time English language instruction, and many leave school without a diploma and several years behind in grade-level attainment.

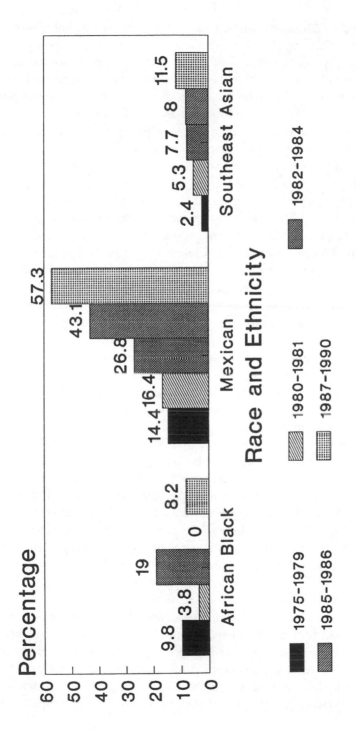

Figure 4.4. Foreign Born Age 17 Neither in School Nor High School Graduates by Cohort and Selected Race-Ethnic Groups, U.S., 1990

SOURCE: U.S. Bureau of the Census (1993b).

Immigrant children from certain groups may also be handicapped by cultural, social, political, and economic contexts. The parents of today's minority youths, especially among Mexican immigrants, often had less formal education than their white and Asian counterparts. Because parents' educational levels are linked to students' academic performance, immigrant minority students from low-income families may start school at a triple disadvantage—being minority, non-English speaking, and poor. As a result, socioeconomic disparities within immigrant minority groups have grown, contributing to increased educational polarization among the second generation.

Students of all ages and from all language groups can suffer from this problem. It is, however, most pronounced among older children, especially those of junior high and high school age, from war-torn areas, and from economically underdeveloped regions. Because immigration is often precipitated by economic desperation and by war or revolution, a high proportion of all immigrant students arrive in the United States with serious educational deficiencies. These deficits may be aggravated by the immigration process, by poor inner-city school systems in the United States, and by the difficult situation of newcomers in a strange country. Although such distress has always been common among immigrants, officials in all districts report that more immigrant students in inner cities are educationally unprepared and their educational deficits are more severe than ever before.

Confounding the problem is that most immigrant children from low-income families have to work (McDonnell & Hill, 1993). Young women 13 or 14 years old may not be expected to earn money outside their homes, but they may be responsible for maintaining the household and caring for younger siblings and cousins while their parents work several jobs. Young men of similar age may be expected by their families to work full-time. Many of the males start to work before they reach the age of 16. Mexican and Central American teenagers are often too mature and carry too many adult burdens to participate in normal secondary school programs. They may have had lives that forced them to adopt adult perspectives permanently.

Immigrant families go through dramatic changes and make enormous efforts in adjustment when they start their new lives in the United States. New lifestyles are mixed, however, with the traditions they brought with them from their homelands. These traditions may conflict with the schedule and the curriculum of western-style U.S. schools. These conflicts often force older youth to make other adjustments.

Among Latin cultures, some girls may be expected to leave school to help their mothers, and pregnant girls may be expected to leave school to raise their babies. Among Southeast Asians, traditions advocate early marriages, early employment of young men, and early childbirth in these young families.

Educational Attainment and Linguistic Status

Many aspects of educational attainment may be related to immigrant children's linguistic status, varying, of course, by ethnicity, socioeconomic status, and other relevant variables. To study the interrelationship of these factors, we have selected one measure of child schooling, school dropouts.

In Chapter 3, we report a positive relationship between English proficiency and family income among foreign-born children. In 1990, among immigrant children speaking a language other than English, two thirds of the children in higher-income families reported oral English proficiency compared to one half of the children in low-income families. In this chapter, our findings support the conventional view that family income is related to school dropout rates. About 22% of foreign-born children aged 16 to 18 from low-income families had not graduated from high school and were not in school in 1990, compared to 16% of those in higher-income families. At each income level, dropout rates decline with an increase in English proficiency. Among the foreign-born children in the low-income group, 74% of youth who reported speaking no English were not in school compared to 12.5% of those who reported speaking English very well. This pattern holds solidly for children at two other higher-income levels. Our findings also support another conventional view that foreign-born children who speak a native tongue may be more likely to become dropouts than children who speak only English (22% vs. 12%, respectively). This pattern also holds for children of all income levels.

When we control simultaneously for English proficiency, for whether children speak other languages, and for family income, however, the school dropout rates for various groups become intriguing. Figure 4.5 shows the general pattern in 1990 for all 16- to 18-year-old foreign-born youth of low and high family income levels and also for Mexican youths. For all foreign-born children, among children who

70

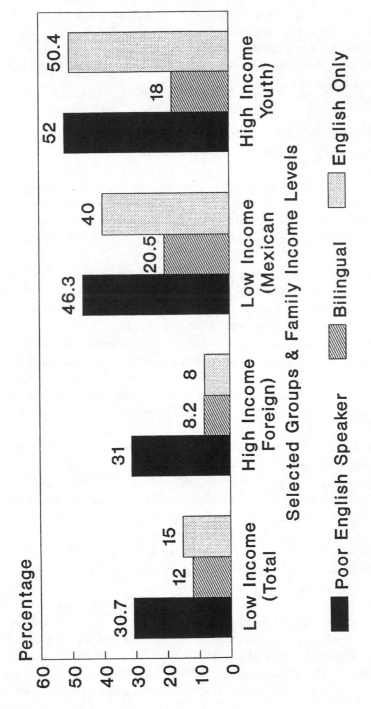

Figure 4.5. School Dropout Rates for Total Foreign-Born and Mexican-Born Youth Aged 16-18 by Linguistic Status and Income, U.S., 1990
SOURCE: U.S. Bureau of the Census (1993b).

were poor English speakers (those who spoke a language other than English at home and did not speak English very well), the school dropout rates are high regardless of the family income (31%). Among children of high-income families, school dropout rates are similar for children who spoke English only and for those who were bilingual speakers (spoke English very well and spoke a language other than English at home). The children of low-income families who reported speaking English very well and also speaking a language other than English at home, however, have lower dropout rates (12%) than do children who spoke English only (15%). The two different patterns by family income level hold for white children from non-English language countries, for African and Caribbean black children, and for Southeast Asian children. Among other Asian children, those who reported speaking English only are less likely to become school dropouts than the bilingual speakers; however, the dropout percentages for all three Asian groups of various linguistic statuses are low (5.5% for poor English speakers, 2.3% for bilingual speakers, and 1.4% for English-only speakers).

This distinction on dropout rates is most remarkable among Hispanic children. The chances of Hispanic children becoming school dropouts are cut in half for bilingual speakers compared to English-only or poor English speakers. Among Mexican children from low-income families, the dropout rate for bilingual speakers is 20% compared to 46% for poor English speakers and 40% for English-only speakers. Among children of high-income families, the dropout rate for bilingual speakers is 18% compared to 52% for poor English speakers and 50% for English-only speakers. Among non-Mexican Hispanic children of low-income families, the dropout rate for bilingual speakers is 10% compared to 27% of poor English speakers and 23% of English-only speakers. Among the children of high-income families, the dropout rate for bilingual speakers is 8% compared to 29% of poor English speakers and 21% of English-only speakers.

For dropouts with less than 5 years of schooling, the contrast is just as compelling. Our findings show that youth of all family income levels who are English-only speakers are more likely to become early dropouts than youth who are bilingual speakers. Among Mexican youths, 7% and 10% of English-only speakers from low- and high-income levels, respectively, are dropouts with less than 5 years education. The dropout rates for poor English speakers are 6% and 7%, respectively, and for bilingual speakers of both income levels, the rate is 1.5%. The

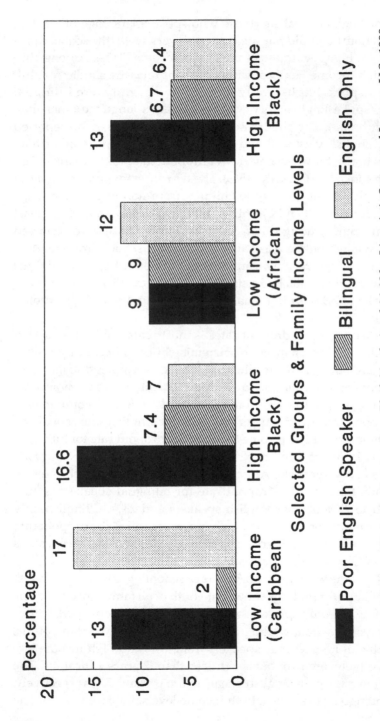

Figure 4.6. School Dropout Rates for Foreign-Born Black Youth Aged 16-18 by Linguistic Status and Income, U.S., 1990
SOURCE: U.S. Bureau of the Census (1993b).

same pattern occurs among other Hispanic groups: 9% and 7% from low- and high-income levels, respectively, are English-only speakers compared to 3% and 4% for poor English speakers.

Black immigrant children showed a slightly different version of the pattern for total foreign-born children. Although the dropout rates for black children of higher-income families are similar to the total foreign-born children (see also Figure 4.5), low-income black children who are English-only speakers are more likely to become dropouts than children who barely speak English. Figure 4.6 reveals that 2% of Caribbean black bilingual speakers are school dropouts compared to 13% of poor English speakers and 17% of English-only speakers. Among black immigrant children from Africa, the dropout rates were 9% for both poor English speakers and bilingual speakers and 12% for English-only speakers.

How can these different patterns of relationship between dropout rates and linguistic status, across various ethnic groups and by family income levels, be explained? One explanation is that this shows the benefits of bilingual experiences for Hispanic children, especially the poor. Other explanations may emphasize effects of racial and class stratification (Portes & Schauffler, 1994) or selective assimilation (Gibson, 1988; Rong, Brown, & Guo, 1996). Gibson has argued for the positive effects of being bicultural and bilinguistic on language minority children's schooling. Rong, Brown, and Guo have argued that the negative effects of rapid Americanization among black immigrant children may lead these children to adapt the inner-city oppositional-antischool culture and therefore drop out of school. Further discussion of Hispanic, Asian, and black immigrant groups is found in Chapters 7, 8, and 9. Before examining each of these groups in detail, we return to issues of explanation by considering in the next two chapters how immigration, acculturation, and responses to schooling have been conceptualized by others seeking to understand and ameliorate the immigrant condition.

5

Learning
New Cultures

People have migrated since before they became homo sapiens. Our hominid ancestors, who evolved in Africa (Leakey & Lewin, 1992), spread to Asia and elsewhere, and homo sapiens has since circled the globe. Much of the prehistoric and historic record centers on migrations of people: many peoples shifting back and forth across the Middle East, the Arabs moving east as well as circling the Mediterranean Sea, the Mongols conquering China, the Norse peoples raiding and settling across Eastern and Western Europe and the North Atlantic lands, and of course the European expansion and colonization of the rest of the globe. Humans have thus always been mobile. Parts of the globe most inaccessible from the African origin—the western hemisphere and Australia, for example—may have been inhabited by a more-or-less single movement of peoples. Even within these areas, however, the archaeological record indicates shifting of peoples. Immigration, then, except for the initial settlement of territories by homo sapiens, is interactive: Immigrants are those moving into an area from elsewhere, and hosts are current inhabitants of the area being moved into.

Host experiences vary. History documents many cases of unwilling hosts, people like the Han in China who initially resisted the Mongols, or the Balkan communities who resisted the Turkish invasions. Hosts have less commonly sought immigrants—the repopulation of Eastern Europe following the depredations of the 14th-century plague, for example. The Arab and European capture and enslavement of Africans, as we have mentioned, is viewed as the forced migration of individuals. Finally, migrations during the modern period have been the movements of individuals and families in comparison to some of the mass migrations of whole communities characterizing the premodern era.

The United States, of course, was built from the European colonization of North America and its subjugation of both the indigenous population who preceded the Europeans and the Africans brought as slaves. More than 65 million people emigrated from Europe to the western hemisphere between the 17th and the 20th centuries; another 20 million people were forcibly removed from Africa to the New World. What has made the United States unique among nation states around the world is its policy toward immigration. Although this policy has varied over time in limits and restrictions, the United States has historically welcomed newcomers. The Statue of Liberty in New York Harbor is as much a symbol of welcome to the destitute, the harried, and the homeless as it is a representation of democratic government.

What causes people to migrate? Some roam as a way of life, although nomads typically move around a fixed territory. Population pressures—too many people for too few resources in a given area—lead some people to search for better opportunities. Others flee the encroachment of armed conquerors seeking plunder or enlargement of their own territory. In historic times, people have migrated to proselytize or to avoid persecution for their religious beliefs. Whether sought or impelled, migration is fraught with hazard, uncertainty, and distress.

Causes and Motivations
for Modern Immigration

The reasons for emigration and immigration and the consequences of these actions in modern times are functions of both economic and individual factors. Lee's (1966) push-and-pull theory focuses on individual decisions: Past immigration movements were explained as the collection of each individual's decisions. More recent applications of Lee's theory, however, incorporate an international labor market redistribution theory, viewing individuals' decisions in a global, social, and economic context. According to this theory, human labor inevitably flows from the market with lower payoffs to the market with higher payoffs. Many scholars believe that the evolution of the world economy has made international migration necessary. World-system theorists argue that markets and trade disrupt traditional economic and social systems, making emigration a natural outgrowth of colonial policies and the activities of multinational businesses (Bloom & Brender, 1993; Martin & Widgren, 1996). This theory explains not only why Mexicans cross the border to the United States, but also why a half-million Turkish and Eastern European workers went to Germany; why Algerians went to France; West Indians to Britain; and Filipinos to Japan, Singapore, and Taiwan.

Today's migration from developing to industrial countries began with demand-pull recruitment of temporary workers from developing countries by employers in industrial countries to fill what was believed to be a temporary need for additional labor. The current labor vacancy list provided by the U.S. Department of Labor shows that the jobs filled by immigrants are highly dichotomized in required skills and education levels: high technology jobs at the top of the pay and status scale and manual labor jobs at the bottom (cf. Lamphere, 1992; Lamphere, Stepick, & Grenier, 1994).

Immigration of Manual Labor Workers

Employers in industrial countries recently have had to recruit migrant workers to fill lower-level or lowest-level jobs: seasonal farm labor, hospitality industry, and other low-paying service work. According to Piore (1979), many such "secondary jobs" cannot be automated or upgraded, creating a persistent need for workers willing to accept these low-wage, low-status jobs. These secondary labor markets could be eliminated, but only at an enormous cost. Some theorists (e.g., Portes & Walton, 1981) believe that the governments of industrial countries do not want to control immigration because the availability of migrant workers helps create competition in the labor market, and this holds down labor costs.

Post-World War II Germany recruited Turkish and southern European "guestworkers." Germany also launched a guestworker program in the 1960s to expand its manufacturing industries. Similarly, the United States helped create a binational labor market with Mexico through the Bracero program, a series of agreements that admitted almost 5 million Mexican farm workers, or Braceros, to the United States temporarily between 1942 and 1964 (Martin & Midgley, 1994).

Several misconceptions have been held about labor arrangements of this kind. First, policymakers assumed that migration would stop if the industrial countries decided to halt labor recruitment. It did not. Migration of Turks to Germany as well as Mexicans to the United States continued. Second, they assumed that temporary workers would leave when the job markets in industrial countries plateaued. These industrial countries soon discovered, however, that nothing is more permanent than temporary foreign workers. Some German and American businesses, accustomed to foreign workers, continued to employ them. Furthermore, years of forces attracting foreign workers had other effects: Countries became accustomed to and reliant on exporting excess labor, helped by the network of friends and families that workers had established in the United States and elsewhere. Another assumption was that jobs held by immigrants would revert to jobs for native-born workers after the immigrants left. When, however, the United States officially ended the Bracero program, the jobs filled by Braceros were eliminated by machines. Similarly guestworker jobs in Europe were eliminated by trade and mechanization after immigrants left. Few instances occurred in which the jobs held by immigrants were filled by unemployed natives (Massey, 1993; Martin & Midgley, 1994).

The labor situation in many developing countries is complicated by the global economic restructuring that shifts jobs from agriculture into more productive industry and service sectors. Between 1950 and 1990, the share of the world labor force in agriculture fell from two thirds to one half. In developing countries, the proportion dropped from four fifths to two fifths. Many migration flows to the industrial countries began when these countries recruited guestworkers stagnating in poor economies—a response to the pull of labor demands. Countries contributing emigrants may also develop a dependency on another country's labor market, both as a source of income when emigrants send back part of their earnings as remittance and as a source of jobs for young workers underemployed at home. Every year the world's migrants send about $70 billion back to their countries of origin (Martin & Widgren, 1996).

Pull and push factors are like the poles of a battery: Without a link between them, they produce no migration. Networks are one major link that turn potential into actual migration. Migration networks enable people to learn about opportunities abroad and to take advantage of them. The most important elements of networks are friends and family members abroad who can provide credible information about jobs and other opportunities, perhaps finance the trip, and often offer shelter after arrival. Labor brokers, smugglers, employers, and migrant organizations can also fulfill these information and placement functions. Relationships established in colonial times, or through the recruitment of guestworkers, explain why more Filipinos migrate to the United States than to Japan or why Turks tend to head for Germany and Moroccans for France. Noneconomic factors, especially networks, explain how the movement of migrants around the globe is not random (Bloom & Brender, 1993).

Immigration of Professionals

Somewhat different patterns explain the immigration of professionals to the United States, a country moving from an industrial to an information society. Human brainpower is replacing the use of human physical labor to create wealth, and the technology of the day extends and enhances mental abilities. Accordingly, U.S. jobs have shifted from blue collar to white collar. Census data in 1930 indicated about 20% of the labor force was in white-collar occupations. The percentage rose to 36% in 1950, 41% in 1960, and 48% in 1970; in 1980 it was above 53%. As the economy grows more complex, it will depend more on human resources and education (Silk, 1988). Gradually, U.S. immigration policy has changed to favor the more educated over those reuniting with family; 20% of immigrants to the United States, excluding refugees, were accepted on the basis of their skills in 1994, compared with 14% in 1992.

As early as 1968, Thomas predicted that contemporary immigration would be characterized by professional elite migration, science-based capital formation, and direct foreign investment. With these economic and social developments, a command market for brainpower was created that transcended state and national boundaries. Immigration became a reasonable and indispensable choice for many people because of the rapid growth of educational and cultural exchanges among nations and the daily expanding international trade. It also became more feasible as communication and transportation improved. Crossing oceans today has become cheaper, quicker, and safer than ever before.

Johnson (1968) has identified two motivations for professional people to move to the United States. First, some immigrants wish to flee oppression; others fear victimization by their governing regimes. Second, in many countries, some western industrial nations among them, an unfavorable labor market permits few opportunities for choice or change of occupation and limits chances for acceptable work. Poorly developed systems of education and rigid social structures further limit social and economic mobility. Also, to a considerable number of professionals, working conditions in their home countries are far from satisfactory. Opportunities to communicate with other professionals and for career advancement may be strictly limited. Anyone wishing for improvement may think about migrating to a more favorable place.

The United States has attracted distinguished professional people from all over the world, including scientists, engineers, economists, administrators of the largest and most innovative companies, fine and performing artists, writers, one joint chief of staff of the military, and two secretaries of state. The United States has benefited from those immigrants' contributions. About half of U.S. Nobel Prize winners are foreign born, and half of those who are not foreign born are the children of foreign-born parents. Of those who are native born, many have had some education abroad. U.S. Nobel Prize winners have been drawn from Germany, Great Britain, France, Switzerland, Sweden, the Netherlands, Denmark, China, Japan, Canada, and Latin America.

The United States could never have developed so sophisticated a level of technology or so high a level of industrialization without continued heavy immigration. Immigration has contributed to the American desire for change and acted as an "equalizer" or "democratizer," producing a less rigid social structure. Immigration, according to Lee (1970), has exerted great influence on the shaping of U.S. social structure, the character of its people, and its culture in general.

The Immigrant's Reception

What has been the experience of immigration for those coming to the United States? Experiences have varied, of course (cf. Goode & Schneider, 1994; Handlin, 1951; Howe, 1980). Some groups—the Irish, the Italians, the Jews from Eastern Europe, most Asians—were denigrated and despised for many years by those native-born Americans who traced their heritage to Anglo-Saxon forebears. Other groups, especially those representing professional classes in their countries of origin, had fewer negative experiences—Cubans fleeing Castro's revolution and Hungarians fleeing the Communist crackdown, for example.

Attitudes toward immigration generally have varied (cf. Macias, 1996). The U.S.'s image of welcoming newcomers is one most Americans, remembering their own roots as immigrants, are especially proud of (Anzovin, 1985). But the U.S. public has simultaneously viewed immigration as imposing grave problems on the economy and has had deep concerns about the political, social, cultural, and language consequences of immigration.

Harwood (1986) and other scholars have found that attitudes toward legal and illegal immigration expressed in polls taken over the past 50 years reflect a commonly held assumption that the immigration of poor and unskilled people imposes a social cost on the United States. This viewpoint has been endorsed by many politicians and a few economists (Chaze, 1985; Heritage Foundation, 1985), but is rejected by most eminent economists and social scientists (Simon, 1984; Thomas, 1954).

Throughout the 19th and into the 20th century, immigrants to the United States were expected to assimilate to mainstream society as quickly as possible. Although ethnic enclaves in cities and even rural areas provided respite, protection, and some maintenance of their original cultures and languages, migrants outside these areas were expected to speak English, conform to mainstream norms and values, and affirm allegiance to the U.S. government (e.g., La Sorte, 1985). The melting pot was the symbol of this experience: Migrants were to lose their distinctive features and melt into the homogeneous culture of the English-speaking, Anglo-Saxon elite.

As we have emphasized, the principal tool of this melting pot assimilation has been the public school. Since the middle of the 19th century, the native born have looked to public education as the primary means of assimilating an increasingly diverse immigrant pool. The relationship, then, between immigration and education in the United States is historical. Those who at present seek to deny public education to the children of illegal immigrants thus are challenging a tradition as old as the nation, and are cunningly striking at the immigrant's traditional means of social mobility—free schooling.

In recent years, the melting pot, assimilationist ideal for bringing diverse peoples together into one national community, has been challenged (Cornbleth & Waugh, 1995; Phelan & Davidson, 1993). One challenge has come from scholars of various ethnic enclaves around the United States. They emphasize the vital and healthy survival of home cultures in these enclaves and the accommodation of immigrants to mainstream culture in ways that allow them to participate across cultures. Cuban Miami is an example of one such group. The metaphor for such immigrant experiences has come to be the salad bowl rather than the melting pot. Individuals from distinctly identifiable ethnic groups participate in a common national citizenry, marketplace, and popular culture while maintaining ethnic religious affiliations, family patterns, and community traditions (e.g., Leonard, 1992).

Another challenge to the melting pot image has come from the United States's historically involuntary minorities—Native Americans, African Americans, and Mexican Americans from the portions of the Southwest annexed by the United States. These groups and those who study them have pointed out the barriers mainstream society has erected to their assimilation and to their equal participation in the economic, political, and sociocultural life of the nation (e.g., Horowitz, 1983). Neither the melting pot nor the salad bowl metaphors work for those forbidden to sit at the dinner table for a meal they may have even cooked; like European medieval serfs, they have been confined "below the salt." The common public education, providing a conduit to social mobility and access to opportunities for many European immigrants, was denied to indigenous minorities (Jacob & Jordan, 1993). Those who were educated at all were schooled in separate, inferior systems until the civil rights movement of the 1950s.

Acculturation, however, is not merely changes in one group (Bohannan, 1995). Acculturation results from sustained contact among two or more groups. It is the exchange and adaptation of practices, beliefs, knowledge, and skills among different groups—the result of the borrowing is a recombining of the old into something new. In a sense, U.S. culture is a result of the acculturation that originated with the European migration and that has continued since then. The United States of 1800, 1900, and 2000 are cultures formed from the amalgamation of those contributing to them. A consideration of immigration at the turn of the 21st century must be viewed within the prism of all the previous migrations that have made the host society what it is.

Acculturation and racial and ethnic identity formation and transformation among immigrant minority children has occurred in the United States, then, within the context of this background. These processes—intertwining with such elements as gender, social class, geographical location, and residential community—dramatically affect immigrant children's adjustment. Racial and ethnic socialization of immigrant minority children shares similarities and differences with the socialization of domestic minority children, as we indicate in this chapter.

Immigration can produce profound psychological distress among even the best prepared and most motivated and under the most receptive circumstances (Igoa, 1995). We present here a cultural-contextual interactive model to illustrate the constant efforts immigrants may have to make to adjust to the larger society: being a member of the category of people of color, facing the discrimination of the dominant white majority; being a member of a minority group, interacting with members of other minority groups; and being a member of a supernationality, collaborating with or otherwise relating to immigrants from the other nationalities grouped under the same umbrella.

The Colorization Experience

One model for describing how many immigrant children accommodate to the racial and ethnic strata of U.S. society by changing status and roles is what we call the colorization experience or what others have labeled racialization (Hatcher & Troyna, 1993). Other theories describing the process of Americanization may have fit the experience of many European immigrants to the United States, but we believe they are insufficient for explaining how a Chinese, a Zambian, an Egyptian, or a Jamaican may become American.

In the United States as well as some other countries around the world, the color of people's skin has become a socially and politically reconstructed attribution rather than a mere biological characteristic (Gregory & Sanjek, 1994; Ogbu, 1988). Although many Americans unquestionably assume that Africans and Asians are people of color, few Americans are aware that many of these immigrants have become "colored" only after they have arrived in the United States. Africans in some parts of Africa and Asians in some parts of Asia may not consider themselves people of color. In home cultures, people may identify themselves by common religious ties, similar ethnic heritages, shared socioeconomic statuses, and even by a common experience of having been colonized by Europeans, but they may lack any experience of identifying themselves and others by skin color and other so-called racial characteristics.

Many immigrant children consequently experience a gap between how they define and think of themselves and how members of their host communities view them—the social attribution of many immigrant children conflicts with their personal sense of self. In experiencing this discontinuity, immigrant children encounter a series of identity transformations—racial and ethnic identity reconstructions—beyond their control or that of their families (e.g., Hendricks, 1974; Hudak, 1993; Perez, 1993). Although the colorization experience may be shared by both immigrant adults and children, the characteristics and difficulties of colorization among children require special attention. Children and youth have concerns of their own and respond to transitions differently than do adults. Being young, they are more flexible and adaptable, but they may also lack means to communicate the problems they perceive and may feel powerless to make changes to cope with problems in their adjustment. Children who immigrate when very young may also experience the conflict of identifying with parents who deny colorization but who cannot protect their children from that which occurs outside the home.

Marginalization and
the Minority Experience

Previous scholars of immigration have characterized the immigrant as "marginalized" and "culturally different," concepts also used in analyzing experiences of indigenous groups—Native Americans, most African Americans, and Mexican Americans of the Southwest. Marginalization refers to the relegation of individuals with a stigmatized group identity to the margins of national life—economically, politically, and socially. Educated or not, the jobs immigrants are able to get are largely rejected by the native-born mainstream. Their political participation is regulated by law; although restrictions may be lifted the longer they remain in the United States, they may not achieve the highest political office and they remain vulnerable to deportation in ways that the native born do not. Social marginalization is enforced by discrimination from and lack of acceptance by the middle class, primarily a European American majority (Suarez-Orozco & Suarez-Orozco, 1995).

Cultural difference refers to lack of access to the language, daily knowledge and common practices, and necessary skills of the mainstream society. In the United States, what is considered cultural difference may be accompanied by lack of economic resources. For many years, the hardships and challenges of the immigrant experience were explained by using these two concepts, marginalization and cultural difference. Newcomers lacked the cultural knowledge and skills to compete in economic and political arenas and were deliberately marginalized by practices of the dominant majority. Although the recent wave of immigrants is vulnerable to these same forces, we believe that other influences, such as racialization, are also at work to complicate the experiences of the newest wave of immigrants to the United States (Skerry, 1993).

Marginalization and what has often been an accompanying cultural difference have contributed to the ghettoization of immigrants throughout U.S. history. In both rural and urban areas, immigrants form geographically bounded communities where the native language is spoken and understood, where home cultural practices and values are honored, and where people with common experiences of the host culture can share resources and support. Regardless of their social statuses in their home societies, immigrants from areas other than northern Europe have shared the experience of belonging to a "minority" group—a group often stigmatized by the European American middle class as different at best and inferior at worst. Group identity then may become an association with others from the same nation or from what the native born consider to be similar. In the past 30 years, this minority group identification has become less national and more regional—centered around what we call supernationalities.

Supernationality and Immigrant Identity

Supernationality, also called emergent ethnicities, is the collective identification and common labeling and stereotyping of groups who shared only a tenuous bond—such as language, some physical feature, or geographic locations—before arriving in the United States. For example, Chinese, Japanese, Vietnamese, and others are put into a larger ethnic category called Asians. People from Jamaica, Haiti, and St. Thomas are labeled Caribbeans. Everyone from Mexico south is lumped together as Hispanics. Like previous generations, these immigrants must respond to the image held by others of their origins, but these origins are increasingly viewed as regional rather than national. People as different as Laotians and Koreans are assumed somehow to hold more in common with each other than with the native-born population, an expectation that flabbergasts, even appalls immigrants. Visiting students, scholars, and business people from Argentina and Brazil find themselves grouped with U.S. Mexican Americans although their ancestry may be traced to European and African origins or Native Americans far south of Mexico (e.g., Margolis, 1994).

The earlier waves of migration, dominated by European groups, brought to the United States peoples often characterized by the nations from which they had come. Italians, Poles, and Greeks, for example, were labeled as such by their native-born hosts. The exception to this attribution by nationality is the labeling by their religious affiliation of Jews, who came predominantly from Europe, often sharing Yiddish as a common language. Most of those who currently migrate see themselves as immigrants from a particular nation.

This attribution of identity by the native-born, predominantly European American middle class places people together who might not otherwise seek out one another. It also raises possibilities of economic and political alliances only now being explored around the country (Espiritu, 1992). Nevertheless, it can be a challenge for any child who, recently emigrated from Ecuador, for example, is suddenly thrust into a group of Spanish speakers whose Spanish is foreign and whose English is incomprehensible.

Summary

Public schoolteachers and other U.S. educators, most of whom are white native borns, who work with children unlike themselves in ethnicity, social class, and culture, need to understand that in a society with increasingly complex racial and ethnic situations, each child faces choices in daily life as a member, simultaneously, of different groups. The cultural-contextual interactive model we have presented reveals the difficulties of children who struggle to balance the temptation of complete and quick Americanization with loyalty to their own cultures, under what may be competing pressures from family, friends, and others in the community. Children are racialized, they are marginalized, and they are associated with others very different from themselves. These difficulties and the transition they represent may involve endless effort, pain, self-struggle, frustration, inner turmoil, instability, restlessness, malaise, and identity collapse among immigrant adults and children. Educators and other agents of U.S. society have choices that may ease the transition or hamper it. Understanding these forces is as relevant to immigrant adults as to the native-born educators to whom we address this book. Educators should help immigrant adults recognize and understand their own problems in the reconstruction of their racial and ethnic identities so that they can assist their children in coping with less rancor with this transition. Adjustment problems of immigrant children often derive from the same source as the problems of their parents. While helping their children, these adults need to deal with their own problems too. Educators should learn to recognize what is occurring to the immigrant children in their classrooms and schools and do what they can to reach out also to the parents and families of these children.

6

Learning
in School

Having considered issues of human migration and acculturation generally, we turn now to the educational aspects of immigrants' acculturation. Our focus is the different ways we may explain and understand the experiences immigrant students have in U.S. schools. Over the past 40 years, educational researchers and other scholars (e.g., Jacob & Jordan, 1993) have tried to explain the differential school performance among groups in society, including immigrant groups (e.g., Gibson & Ogbu, 1991), with a variety of theories. We present and discuss the range of theories, including two discredited explanations that still appeal to some seeking simplistic rationalizations. The theories include the biological explanation, the cultural deprivation explanation, the cultural difference explanation, the cultural ecological explanation, the sociocultural (re)productive explanation, and the constructivist explanation. We both find that the experiences of immigrant children in U.S. schools are best understood by using some combination of the last four theories, a cultural-contextual interactive approach.

The Biological Explanation

The biological explanation for the school performance of immigrant children is rooted in 19th-century notions of race. People around the world were categorized into different racial groups and were considered beneficiaries of varying abilities. Contemporary biologists and geneticists have rejected these ideas for many reasons (cf. Gregory & Sanjek, 1994; Konner, 1982).

First, all humans belong to a single species and share a common gene pool. Interbreeding along the edges of all human populations, however isolated they may have been temporarily, has resulted in what are overwhelmingly shared qualities. Second, and related to the first, variations within groups are far greater than between-group variations. What this means is that all humans, however they are grouped overall, exhibit the range of traits from skin color to height and weight to behavioral abilities. Although the public continues to use racial terms such as black and white here in the United States, these designations represent factors more cultural than biological, and they ignore completely the mixed African, European, and Native American heritage of many U.S. citizens. Finally, the traits related to school performance are so complex and so environmentally interactive that they defy a unitary genetic explanation; exactly how genetic inheritance affects human behavior remains a puzzle to be solved. Although people who are not specialists in the study of human genetics periodically revive the genetic argument to explain the varying school performance of children in different groups (e.g., Herrnstein & Murray, 1994), such work has consistently been debunked by researchers (e.g., Fraser, 1995).

The Cultural Deprivation Explanation

A second explanation for differing school performance among the groups in U.S. society was fashionable in the 1960s, the cultural deprivation theory. Just as stereotypic as the genetic explanation, this theory asserts that poor people lack the economic and social resources to develop and maintain any culture and that their children fail in school because they come from homes lacking culture (Collins, 1988).

Needless to say, this was quickly challenged by cultural anthropologists and urban sociologists who have documented the rich cultural lives of both the rural and urban poor in the United States (Valentine, 1968). Human beings produce culture everywhere in the world; what may appear to the outsider as the most meager of material resources is sufficient for people to produce the wealth in cultural variations that has been documented over the past century. Only those few humans raised in isolation from all other humans fail to produce culture; this is because culture is learned and because each human learns culture in interaction with other humans (Carrithers, 1992).

We describe and challenge these well-discredited explanations for differing school performance because sometimes they are used in schools as ways to dismiss children's needs for attention and consideration. All children come to school with different skills, abilities, and knowledge; these vary by experiences and perhaps even by genetic inheritance from individual to individual—although not by group to group. Like the native born, immigrant children arrive at school well cultured and well endowed with variable talents and abilities.

Cultural Difference Theory

How, then, can we understand the differing responses to education and schooling of children from varying groups? A third, helpful explanation for variation in the school performance of children by group is the cultural differences explanation (e.g., Erickson, 1987; McDermott, 1987; Trueba, 1988). Long advocated by educational anthropologists and other scholars, this theory emphasizes that all schools themselves represent a culture. Schools have an institutional culture, and this institutional culture is permeated by influences from the cultures that form its environment. Public schools in the United States have cultures broadly representative of both national and community cultures. Private schools may, in addition, be affected by such factors as religious subcultures if they are parochial or by economic subcultures if they serve, for example, the elite.

All children arrive at school with some acculturation to be managed (Ogbu, 1982). Children with no preschool experience must navigate the challenges of a new institutional culture as they move from home environments to a formal bureaucratic environment. Most children find many adjustments required as they encounter others from different socioeconomic, religious, ethnic, and purportedly racial backgrounds. When the cultures that dominate the school are different from and especially inconsistent with home cultures, children from those home cultures may have difficulty in school performance. The cultural difference theory accounts for differential school performance by emphasizing the difference between school culture and children's home cultures (e.g., Heath, 1983). This theory has been supported in some studies of children from marginalized groups, including immigrants (Delgado-Gaitan & Trueba, 1991).

Children from some groups, especially from some immigrant groups, have, however, consistently done well in school. Many of the children of Jewish immigrants, for example, have a history of high educational achievement regardless of how different their parents' home cultures were from the U.S. culture they migrated into. In this case, the cultural difference theory has been modified to distinguish between differences that conflict and differences that complement; the idea is that some varying home cultures may be different from school culture but share enough common norms and values so that children's adjustment from home to school is facilitated rather than hindered. This means, for educators of all children and especially immigrant children, attending to the cultures children bring to school with them. Are these cultures compatible with school culture? Incompatible with it? How is each child managing the varying influences?

Nevertheless, the pattern remains that many immigrant children and children of immigrants outperform the native born in U.S. schools. The argument is that if school performance were obstructed by conflicting home and school cultures, then this could not occur. By the late 1970s, the cultural difference model had been found to explain some cases but not others.

Cultural Ecological Theory

John Ogbu (1978, 1987), a Nigerian schooled in the United States, has developed what he calls a cultural ecological theory of differing school performance. He considers how culture interacts with the rest of the environment, especially economic and historical factors, to privilege some groups and not others. He examined the variety of different groups marginalized across societies of the world for their different adaptation patterns—for example, assimilation, accommodation, and separatism—in various historical periods to explain the different extent of their success in school and in the larger society. He has divided marginalized groups into the voluntary and involuntary. Voluntary minority groups are those who migrate willingly from one environment to another. Involuntary minorities are those incorporated into society by force; as we have noted, in the United States, this includes African

Americans, Native Americans, and the Mexican Americans living in territories annexed into the United States. Ogbu found that around the world involuntary minorities had problems in schools whereas voluntary minorities did not; he explains this pattern by pointing to different environmental factors and the interaction of the environmental factors with people's expectations of what is possible to achieve. Many, but not all, people from involuntary minority groups, with a history of prejudice, discrimination, and enforced poverty, view school as another means of oppression rather than as an avenue to economic and social mobility. Likewise, most people from voluntary groups consider education and schooling to be a route to a better life; they press their children to perform well, and their children may outperform the native born in many societies.

Ogbu's theory, still argued and debated among scholars, provided an explanation for how some groups of children, whose family cultures were very different from the European American culture that dominates U.S. schools, have nevertheless performed well in these schools (cf. Goto, 1997). What this means for educators is that economic and historical relationships must be considered along with social and cultural influences. Voluntary, semivoluntary, and involuntary or caste-like immigrants are likely to have different experiences in the United States. Voluntary immigrants, those who have a viable choice of immigrating or remaining in their home societies, may often be people who feel they have the most control over their lives and futures and who master school competencies with confidence. Semivoluntary immigrants are those fleeing some situation in their native societies that prevents them from returning—warfare and violence or political and economic oppression. Semivoluntary immigrants, such as the Cuban Americans who fled the Castro revolution, seek asylum elsewhere and arrive there motivated by feelings of relief or even gratitude. Involuntary or caste-like immigrants are those oppressed by economic and social barriers in their native societies who may also be fleeing such circumstances, who are being literally pushed out of their home areas. Population pressures in parts of rural Mexico, for example, operate among the most poverty stricken to push people north; many risk the fears of border crossings regularly just to keep themselves and their families fed. Finally, whether people migrated to the United States in a first wave of movement versus the later waves also affects their acculturation. Among those fleeing disruption, initial groups are often the wealthier and better educated in their home societies. Once these folks leave, those who follow often lack such resources.

These differing experiences lead to differing responses by immigrants to the host culture. Some immigrants seek to assimilate to whatever they see as the most dominant group—middle-class, European American in the United States, for example. As we have noted previously, this classic assimilation or melting pot model was the common expectation of immigrants in the 19th century. Urban schools of that era were often organized to Americanize the children of immigrants sufficiently to provide an adequate labor supply for U.S. industry, and many immigrants of that time were limited in their mobility to working-class occupations and neighborhoods. The economic structures in place in the United States thus limited assimilation to the middle class unless people were able to find some means of access such as higher education or political activity. Partly as a result of such restrictions, groups responded with nonassimilation or even separatism. Some first-generation immigrants avoided learning English, for example. Many people gathered in neighborhoods and communities of folk from the same nation, and across the United States, Little Italys, Chinatowns, and such were formed. These immigrant communities can even be found in rural areas of the Midwest and the Far West. Consequently, assimilation and nonassimilation can be considered culturally and structurally. The economic and political structures in place in the United States can facilitate or hinder assimilation, and hence prompt nonassimilation, at least for a generation or two. Cultural assimilation may or may not accompany structural assimilation; many of those who refused to learn English were also limited to manual labor and hence were neither culturally nor structurally assimilated to the dominant middle-class group.

Cultural assimilation is the extent that immigrants adopt the language and customs (housing, food, clothing, religions, and so forth) of the host country. Language resources (English attainment, native language attrition and retention) and year of residence in the host country are two measures representing a person's cultural assimilation. Structural assimilation is the extent to which immigrants integrate themselves into educational, political, and social institutions. Educational attainment, income, and occupation in the host country are generally viewed as major indicators of immigrants' structural assimilation. Completion of high school can be viewed as important evidence of an immigrant youth's structural assimilation. A positive relationship between cultural assimilation and school attainment is generally assumed in research literature: Mastering English can help immigrants to succeed in school, employment, and other career-related promotions.

This assumption, however, is increasingly facing challenges from multiculturalism. Many recent studies indicate that cultural assimilation does not necessarily guarantee structural assimilation, and structural assimilation is not fully dependent on cultural assimilation (Ogbu & Matute-Bianchi, 1986). The history of immigration to the United States is full of legends of self-made individuals, but the stories of recent immigrants are likelier to reveal a polarization: the richer doing well, but the poorer staying poor. Researchers have reported that education and social status in home countries help some immigrants, such as those from Cuba, Hong Kong, Taiwan, and countries in South America, to carry their social connections, wealth, and human capital into the new world (Barringer, Gardner, & Levin, 1993; Gardner, Robey, & Smith, 1985). When these people settle in middle-class neighborhoods, their children may enroll in schools that receive them enthusiastically and provide them with ESL and other needed services. These parents may pay for after-school tutoring and other outside-school help. Even if the children are recent immigrants who speak little English, the chance for them to complete high school and enter college is still very high.

In contrast, some immigrant youth, such as Mexicans or some Southeast Asians, who have resided in the United States for a long time, may speak no English and have little opportunity to be acculturated because they have resided or worked in ethnic neighborhoods and attended schools offering little help in improving their English proficiency. They may flunk courses, remain below grade for their age, be absent frequently, and finally drop out. Furthermore, as Ogbu's theory explains, those immigrants who speak English well may still drop out of school because they are discouraged by the negative educational or employment experience of others of the same ethnic group; they do not see any payoff from a high school diploma. Or in some cases, they cannot afford to stay in school after the age of 16.

An alternative to assimilation is separatism. Separatism is a voluntary or forced separation of a group from the rest of society. Of course, no group living in the United States is completely cut off from the economic and social life of the nation. Even groups most isolated, such as the Amish who migrated from northern Europe, have some avenues of intercourse with the broader society (Hostetler & Huntington, 1971). Separatism is a matter of degree, and this position is very controversial in U.S. society. The right of such separatist communities to educate their young themselves has been debated through the middle of this century. The most egregious examples of separatism in the United States have been the forced segregation of African Americans, Native Americans, and Mexican Americans from the resources and decision-making accessible to all others (cf. Menchaca & Valencia, 1990).

More common recently than separatism is what Margaret Gibson (1988) first labeled accommodation, the selective adaptation and rejection of varying elements of U.S. culture by immigrant groups (cf. McNall, Dunnigan, & Mortimer, 1994). In studying a Sikh group in a small town in California, Gibson documented this pattern of selection. The group sought to acquire education for their children while controlling the youngsters' access to the peer culture so prevalent in U.S. schools. Economic mobility was gained, despite some structural barriers, by cooperation in the Sikh community and by sheer hard work. Overall, adults in the group tried to navigate the structural barriers to economic success while maintaining traditional cultural patterns at home and within the immigrant community.

Sociocultural (Re)production Theories

An alternative to the assimilation-accommodation-separatism models for acculturation are the social and cultural production and reproduction models used to explain individuals' responses to schooling and to barriers to mobility by race, class, and gender among the native born in many countries. These sociocultural (re)production models all view schools as major agents of the transmission of socially stratified roles in society (Goetz & Grant, 1988; Levinson, Foley, & Holland, 1996; McCarthy & Apple, 1988). In schools, students learn which group society assigns them to and how to behave appropriately in that group. Either conformity or resistance may yield similar results of keeping students in the groups to which they are ascribed. Conformity is the acceptance of these expectations, but resistance to the school culture and the designated ascriptions may also leave the status quo intact. To the extent that students resist and rebel against strictures of school personnel, they relegate themselves to educational failure and to reinforcing stereotypes charged against them. An example of how resistance works in U.S. schools is the epithet of "acting white" charged against high-achieving African American students by their fellows; the culture of U.S. schools, viewed as representing European American domination, is resisted by students who view this avenue of social mobility as betraying their racial identity (Fordham, 1996).

Sociocultural (re)production theory helps explain the school failure that has developed among some immigrant students in the United States and elsewhere (Solomon, 1992). To the extent that the category of racially different is ascribed to immigrants, they are set up for a society that stratifies nonwhites or people of color for lower-socioeconomic status. Thus, colorization puts a glass ceiling on immigrants' social mobility.

Constructivism

A final theory that addresses the acculturation of immigrant children in U.S. schools is constructivism (Fosnot, 1996). This theory has developed from international scholarship on the interaction of children's social and psychological development. Humans are viewed as active selectors and builders of knowledge through their interaction with others, their reflection on such interactions, and their attempts to relate developing ideas both to previously learned ones and to those held by others. Cultural transmission in this view is not merely acceptance of what is known by others but an engagement with others that involves perceiving and matching perception to what is already known, grappling with confusions and conflicts, building meaning from these processes, and trying out the personally developed meaning in discourse with others. Constructivism is one powerful explanation for cultural change because knowledge is not moved from one generation to the next unchanged but is transformed by each generation of thinkers and interacters as they struggle to learn from their forebears and to teach their descendants. Constructivism, because of its focus on the individual-in-interaction and the group-as-interacting-individuals, is a way to explain how people are multicultural rather than monocultural. People are learning and transforming cultures in multiple arenas, and individuals take what they have learned in one setting to affect what and how they learn in other settings. Bilingualism and biculturalism, therefore, may help immigrant children manage the barriers of racial discrimination, limited resources, and the pressure of anglicization. Constructivism explains how some immigrant children have established links between their new world and the social-institutional knowledge from the worlds they left behind. This is a process of construction, deconstruction, and reconstruction.

In the following three chapters we consider patterns of acculturation shared by immigrant children from three supernational groups: Hispanic, Asian, and black. To interpret the patterns we have discovered in the 1990 census data, we use the cultural-contextual interactive approach we have described in Chapters 5 and 6.

7

Hispanic
Children

Hispanics are a sizable and fast growing part of the U.S. population. They represent an increasing proportion of the nation's labor force and an important human resource. As we have already observed, the largest proportion of new immigrants in the 1980s and 1990s were Hispanics (Conley & Baumann, 1993; Spring, 1994). Because of high immigration rates, higher birthrates, and relative youth, the Hispanic population increased more than seven times as rapidly as other groups between 1980 and 1990.

According to census data (Hirschman, 1994), of the 22 million Hispanic Americans in 1990, the largest groups were Mexican Americans of more than 13 million (more than 60%), Puerto Ricans (2.7 million), Cubans (1 million), Dominicans (0.5 million), Central Americans (1.3 million), South Americans (1 million), and generic categories of Spaniard, Spanish, and Spanish American (1.1 million). The census bureau's 1992 middle-series projections (Del Pinal, 1993) suggest that rapid growth of the Hispanic population may continue into the 21st century, with anticipated increases from 22.4 million (or 9% of the population) in 1990 to 39 million (or 13%) by 2010. By then, Hispanics will surpass blacks as the largest minority group in the United States.

Youth of Hispanic origin make up increasingly large proportions of the nation's students; they are becoming a majority among U.S. minority students. The influx of Hispanics has been particularly dramatic in the Southwest, where in some public school districts Spanish-speaking students comprise the majority. Today, nearly one half of the children entering kindergarten in the nation's two largest school districts—Los Angeles Unified and New York City—come from Hispanic homes. Because of these population shifts, U.S. schools must respond promptly; increases in the enrollment of Hispanic students raise questions about their attainment and the adequacy of U.S. schools for meeting their needs.

Immigration, especially emigration from Mexico to the United States, is a contested political issue (Davis, 1990). Some communities have welcomed immigrants and their children and have appreciated the vitality and cultural diversity they bring to schools (e.g., Peshkin, 1991). In other locales, their arrival arouses fear that youth from immigrant communities may drain already scarce school resources or compete with U.S.-born natives in job training and career development programs (Stewart, 1993). Where immigrant settlement has been significant, new residents have sometimes encountered negative responses from longer-term U.S. residents. These negative responses include attempts to exclude children of illegal immigrants from public schools in Texas and Florida in the late 1970s; opposition to bilingual programs; the movement for the establishment of English as the only official language; and the 1994 passage in California of Proposition 187, which seeks to limit the education and health services provided to undocumented immigrants and their children. These actions target Mexican immigrant children and their families (Rong & Grant, 1995).

English acquisition and Spanish attrition and retention have become the focus of a heated debate. The debate extends well beyond the boundary of language, however, to the areas of ethnic socialization of Hispanic children and rising multiculturalism and pluralism in the United States.

This chapter examines several issues on the education of Hispanic immigrant children. In the first section, we analyze census data to present a demographic profile of Hispanic immigrant children, including country-of-origin, language resources and usage, year of entry, and family type and income. In the second section, we use census data to address two questions: How do the five major Hispanic groups differ educationally, and how does their attainment differ from Asian and black immigrant children? Second, how severe is the dropout problem among Mexican and Central American children? We also consider whether Spanish usage among Hispanic children affects their educational attainment, and if so, how? This section emphasizes the differences among the various nationality groups entering the United States under different conditions and with very different experiences and histories. We then present Hispanic children's educational enrollment and school completion, focusing on the school dropout problem and illiteracy. This information is discussed in the context of their language facility and is compared by national origins across cohorts. Finally, the discussion section offers recommendations for educators who wish to function effectively in educating Hispanic immigrant children.

Intraethnic Differences

Although labels such as "Hispanic" are, of course, umbrella terms for large groups of persons who differ substantially among themselves, these groups are often regarded in research and theory as homogeneous (e.g., Waggoner, 1991). More recent research, however, recognizes that intraethnic differences within broad ethnic classifications occur and therefore treats Hispanics instead as a polarization: Cubans and Mexicans. This research indicates that persons who are descendants of Cubans have had higher education and socioeconomic attainment in the United States than persons tracing descent to Mexico or Puerto Rico (Suarez-Orozco, 1987, 1989). Not only did the former group enter the United States as voluntary or refugee immigrants rather than as indigenous minorities, but they also entered with greater English language proficiency and higher parental socioeconomic and educational status. Central American children have not received much research attention until recently, and they have been put into categories either with Cubans or with Mexicans, depending on how well people believe they do in schools. Studies on South American immigrant children are almost nonexistent. Hirschman and Falcon (1985), who pooled several years' data from the General Social Survey to create a sample large enough to analyze intraethnic differences among Hispanic children, found higher educational attainment rates among persons of Central and South American ancestry, compared to those of Mexican or Puerto Rican descent. The two-group classification, however, may also mask intragroup differences. More recent studies that concentrate on specific nationality groups within the Hispanic population and focus on a single group suggest a social-demographic gap between people from countries in Central America and people from South America or Cuba (Carrasquillo, 1991; Chinchilla, Hamilton, & Loucky, 1993; Melville, 1985; Stepick & Grenier, 1993; U.S. Bureau of the Census, 1993a). Research (e.g., Matthijs, 1996) also suggests that Dominicans—Spanish-speaking blacks—had fewer years of schooling and lower labor market payoff from their education than other immigrants and native blacks. These studies suggest that, wherever possible, it is important to compare attainment of groups within broadly defined ethnic categories. Fortunately, the very large sample used in this study permits further divisions within the two broadly defined Hispanic groups.

Demographic Profile of Hispanic Immigrant Children

Researching Hispanic students' education is complex because of the diversity of Hispanic peoples from many nationalities, who may be connected only by similarity in language. Hispanic as a supernationality is an artificially constructed category including people of all races, various cultures, and residency across broad geographic areas. Beyond language, for example, little is held in common between Cuban and Mexican Americans. Cubans, who are mostly white and professional, have escaped a communist regime and settled in the United States as refugees. Mexican Americans have entered the United States under completely different conditions. A large number of Mexicans "became" U.S. citizens in the 19th century because of Mexico's defeat in the Mexican American war. A considerable number of Mexicans recently have entered the United States legally and illegally. The latter has overshadowed the image of legal Mexican immigrants. Endless battles about the rights to be educated and to be educated in both English and Spanish have ended in the courts.

In this chapter we subdivide Hispanics into five groups, tracing ancestry to the following countries or regions: Central America, Cuba, Mexico, South America, and the Dominican Republic. The foreign-born Hispanic population aged 5-18 has the following composition by national origin: 140,000 Central Americans (43% Salvadoran, 23% Nicaraguan, 17% Guatemalan, 9% Honduran, and 8% Panamanian or other Central American); 25,000 Cubans; 36,000 Dominicans; 550,000 Mexicans; and 60,000 South Americans (35% Colombian, 22% Peruvian, 15% Ecuadorian, and 28% Chilean, Argentinean, or other South American). Puerto Ricans are excluded here, because almost all (99%) Puerto Ricans are classified as native born, Puerto Rico being a U.S. territory. European Hispanics are also excluded in this analysis.

To simplify subsequent text and tables, we refer to Hispanic groups by country of origin—for example, Cuban, Mexican—although most so labeled are actually Cuban American, Mexican American, and so forth. We refer to non-Hispanic whites simply as whites.

At an income level of $25,000, Dominican immigrant children come from families with the lowest income of all Hispanic groups and also the lowest of all 15 race, ethnic, and nationality groups we have discussed. Mexican families have the next lowest income at $26,000; slightly higher are Central American families ($29,000) and Cuban families ($29,100). The families of South American children have the highest income, at $34,000. Family incomes of most Hispanic groups are lower than those of Jamaican, African, and most of the Asian groups except Southeast Asians.

Mexican, Dominican, and Central American children live in families far below the poverty line. In family income and poverty status, Hispanic groups have the fewest resources of all foreign-born children except Southeast Asians.

Among children who live with parents, 78% of Cuban children live with two parents, as do 74% of Mexican children, 72% of South American children, and 68% of Central American children. Of Dominican immigrant children, 50% live with two parents (40% live with their mothers), and that percentage is lowest among all immigrant groups; however, it is higher than some of the native-born groups, such as native-born blacks. Of Central Americans, 14% live with their fathers, the second highest among all immigrant groups, the highest being the Haitian children. Living with fathers may be related to being very recent immigrants; the hardships before and during immigration often set families apart.

By far, Central American children have the most recent immigration experience. In 1990, 61% of Central American children had immigrated to the United States within the past 5 years; 40% of them had resided in the United States less than 3 years. Mexican and Dominican immigrants also have a relatively recent immigration history. Half of them had resided in the United States for less than 5 years, and more than a third had lived in the country for less than 3 years. Although the majority of Mexican Americans are native born, foreign-born Mexican children are more likely than either Cuban and South American immigrant children to be the most recent immigrants in their communities. Two thirds of Cuban and South American foreign-born children came to this country before 1985, and only one in five came to the United States between 1987-1990. The newcomer status of recent immigrants may partially explain low family income and the single parenting of Dominican and Central American immigrant children.

Only about 3% of children who entered the United States between 1987 and 1990 in each of the five Hispanic groups use English as the only language in the home; the vast majority speak a language other than English. Among these children, 1 in 3 South American children; 2 in 10 Dominican, Cuban, and Central American children; and 1 in 10 Mexican children reported speaking English very well. Among the same cohort, 2 of 3 Mexican, Dominican, and Central American children lived in a linguistically isolated household. Among the most recent immigrants, three quarters of the Cuban children live in a linguistically isolated household, compared to half of the South American children.

A study focusing on Hispanic youth, aged 15-24, using a sample that matches the parents and children in the same household (Rong & Grant, 1995), indicates sharp distinctions across Hispanic groups in proportion to U.S. residents who are immigrants, ranging from three quarters of Central Americans being foreign born, to a low one quarter of Mexican youth being foreign born. Rong and Grant's study also reveals variations in mean educational level of heads of household across both nationality subgroups and immigration generations. Dominican and Mexican parents have the lowest levels of education in all immigrant generations, compared to other Hispanic groups and whites from other non-English-speaking countries.

Although previous studies typically combined Central Americans, Cubans, and South Americans into one category, the demographic information in Rong and Grant's study (1995) shows the former group significantly differs from the latter two groups. Immigrant Central Americans are more likely to have parents with fewer years of schooling, to live in a linguistically isolated household, and to have English proficiency problems. Researchers (e.g., Chinchilla, Hamilton, & Loucky, 1993) also have explored the various problems they may have before, during, or after their immigration. The majority of Central Americans who came to the United States in the 1980s fled war and deteriorating economic conditions. A very high proportion of them were undocumented.

Educational Attainment

Research using a variety of data sources suggests that on measures of attainment and persistence in schooling, Hispanics compare unfavorably with non-Hispanic whites or youth of Asian descent and equally or unfavorably with blacks and Native Americans (Arias, 1986; Matute-Bianchi, 1986; Spring, 1994; Valverde, 1987; Velez, 1989). As numerous scholars have noted, however, much of the research on Hispanic attainment in schools has failed to distinguish among heterogeneous groups of differing ethnicity and national origin (e.g., Pedraza, 1991; Portes & Rumbaut, 1996; Suarez-Orozco, 1987).

Many U.S. schoolteachers presume that Mexican and immigrant parents have low educational aspirations for their daughters—marrying and raising children being the objective. Rong and Grant (1995) report, however, that among youth aged 15-24, Hispanic girls have as many or more years of schooling than boys and also higher high school graduation rates.

Enrollment and School Completion

Among children aged 6-16 in 1990, Hispanic children as a group had the highest percentage (12%) not enrolled in school, and this percentage was four times that of Asian children and non-Hispanic whites who came from English-speaking countries. For specific Hispanic groups, it was 6% for South American children and 8% for Dominican, Cuban, and Central American children. Hispanic children are less likely than other children to be in private schools. Six percent of Cuban, South American, and Dominican immigrant children; 3% of Central American children; and 2% of Mexican immigrant children were in private schools in 1990, compared to 17% of non-Hispanic white children and 12% of Japanese and Filipino immigrant children.

Among foreign-born children aged 12-18, Table 7.1 indicates that Mexican and Central American children have the lowest percentage (94%) of 5-year elementary school completion, compared to 99% of Cubans, 98% of South Americans, and 97% of Dominican children. Among immigrant children aged 14-18, 77% of South American, 76% of Cuban,

TABLE 7.1 Rates of Elementary, Middle, and High School
Completion by Ethnic-Nationality, U.S., 1990
(in percentages)

	Elementary (5 Years) Age 12-18	Middle (8 Years) Age 14-18	Secondary (12 Years) Age 18
Total native born	96	71	45
Total foreign born	95	68	31
White[a]	99	80	65
White[b]	98	78	49
Haitian	97	77	34
Jamaican	98	78	42
African[c]	98	78	45
Mexican	93	63	18
Dominican	97	73	23
Cuban	99	76	30
Central American	94	66	20
South American	98	77	43
Chinese	99	78	43
Japanese	98	79	39
Korean	99	81	37
Asian Indian	99	78	62
Filipino	98	78	47
Southeast Asian[d]	97	73	26

NOTE: Data U.S. Bureau of the Census (1993b).
a. Non-Hispanic whites who came from countries where English was the
dominant and official language.
b. Non-Hispanic whites who came from countries where English was not the
dominant language.
c. African blacks include blacks from any country on the African continent.
d. Southeast Asian includes Cambodians, Laotians, Hmong, and Vietnamese.

73% of Dominican, 66% of Central American, and 63% of Mexican children completed 8 years of schooling. The middle school completion rate for native-born children is 71%, and for all foreign-born children is 68%. As we have noted previously, at the secondary level a large discrepancy occurs between the high school completion rates of Hispanic groups and those of native-born and foreign-born children. At age 18, all Hispanic groups have lower high school completion rates than native-born children (45%), and all Hispanic groups except South

Americans, with a 43% completion rate, have lower completion rates than total foreign-born youth (31%). The completion rate for immigrant Mexican children is only 18% and is not much higher for Central American youth (20%) or Dominican youth (23%). The percentage is significantly higher for Cuban American youth (30%), but still slightly lower than the completion rates for all foreign-born 18-year-olds.

The lower graduation rate among 18-year-old Hispanic immigrant youth can be explained by several factors. One is that Mexican children usually first go to school at age 7 or 8; therefore, if they graduate, they may graduate from high school later than 18 or 19. Higher dropout rates at all levels of education may be another factor.

Table 7.2 indicates that with dropout rates of 34% among 17-year-olds and 48% among 18-year-olds, Mexican youth have the highest dropout rates of any nationality group, and Central Americans have the second highest dropout rate, 22% for 17-year-olds and 35% for 18-year-olds. Given their low family income, the dropout rates among Dominicans are moderate, 14% for 17-year-olds and 21% for 18-year-olds. Although both Cuban and South American youth have dropout rates lower than the total foreign-born youth population, 16% for 17-year-old and 14% for 18-year-old Cubans, only South American youth have lower dropout rates, 6% for 17-year-olds and 13% for 18-year-olds, than U.S. native-born youth, 9% for 17-year-olds and 12.5% for 18-year-olds. Mexican youth have the greatest illiteracy problem among dropout youth. Of Mexican immigrant youth, 4% of 17-year-olds and 6% of 18-year-olds had less than 5 years of education and were not enrolled in school in 1990. Between 7,000 and 10,000 Mexican foreign-born youth aged 17 and 18 who are not in school each year may never have been in school; they may be functional illiterates in both English and Spanish. The percentages for Central Americans were next highest, 3% for 17-year-olds and 4% for 18-year-olds.

Education, Linguistic Status, and Adaptation

Length of U.S. residence is often used as an indicator to suggest the degree and extent of an immigrant's assimilation. The general assumption is that living in the United States longer results in better spoken English skills while causing the loss of native tongues. Thus, English proficiency, household linguistic isolation status, and the status of speaking a native tongue other than English is used to examine this

TABLE 7.2 School Dropouts by Ethnic-Nationality and Education
Level, U.S., 1990

	Age	Non-High School Dropouts[a] (in percentages)	Dropouts (in percentages)	
			< 5 Years	≥ 5 Years
Total native born	17	90.8	0.2	9.2
	18	87.5	0.3	12.2
Total foreign born	17	82.0	1.7	16.3
	18	74.3	2.7	23.0
White[b]	17	95	0	5
	18	95	0	5
White[c]	17	91	0	9
	18	89	1	1
Haitian	17	93	1	6
	18	92	0	8
Jamaican	17	90	1	9
	18	88	0	12
African Black[d]	17	90	1	9
	18	89	1	9
Mexican	17	66	4	30
	18	52	6	42
Dominican	17	86	1	13
	18	79	1	20
Cuban	17	84	1	15
	18	86	0	14
Central American	17	78	3	19
	18	65	4	31

assimilation among various Hispanic groups and to assess how the patterns may vary.

For all Hispanic groups, length of U.S. residence significantly promotes English proficiency, although each at a different pace. In 1990, among the cohort who came to the United States between 1987 and 1990, 13% of Mexicans, 20% of Dominicans, 17% of Cubans and Central Americans, and 32% of South Americans reported spoken English proficiency. The percentages increase dramatically for the cohort who came to this country between 1975 and 1979; 69% of Mexicans, 75% of Dominicans, 86% of Cubans, 78% of Central Americans, and 83% of South

TABLE 7.2 *Continued*

	Age	Non-High School Dropouts[a] (in percentages)	Dropouts (in percentages)	
			< 5 Years	≥ 5 Years
South	17	94	0	6
American	18	87	0	12
Chinese	17	96	0	4
	18	96	0	4
Japanese	17	97	0	3
	18	97	0	3
Korean	17	95	0	5
	18	95	0	5
Asian Indian	17	97	0	3
	18	98	0	2
Filipino	17	94	0	6
	18	93	0	7
Southeast Asian[e]	17	94	1	5
	18	92	1	7

NOTE: Data from U.S. Bureau of the Census (1993b).
a. Non-high school dropouts indicate persons who either graduated from high school or still were in school.
b. Non-Hispanic whites who came from countries where English was the dominant and official language.
c. Non-Hispanic whites who came from countries where English was not the dominant language.
d. African blacks include blacks from any country on the African continent.
e. Southeast Asian includes Cambodians, Laotians, Hmong, and Vietnamese.

Americans reported proficiency in speaking English. Among all Hispanic groups, Cuban immigrant youth show the largest improvement by far—a 500% increase—in their English proficiency between the 1975 cohort and the 1987 cohort.

The percentage of children who live in linguistically isolated households has also steadily and significantly declined, along with increasing length of the U.S. residency for all Hispanic groups. Among the cohort who came to the United States between 1987 and 1990, 74% of Cubans, 67% of Mexicans, 64% of Central Americans, 62% of Dominicans, and 53% of South American children lived in a linguistically isolated household in 1990. The figures for the cohort who came to this country between 1975 and 1979 and were still living in linguistically isolated households in 1990 are only 14% of South American, 18% of Dominican, 19% of Central American, 22% of Cuban, and 24% of Mexican immigrant children.

These data indicate a tendency toward more English language usage and linguistic adaptation, but not toward English monolingualism. Instead, the tendency is toward bilingualism, a common situation among first-generation immigrants. Almost all Hispanic immigrant children who came to the United States between 1987 and 1990 reported speaking Spanish at home: 98% of Dominican, Central American, and South American children; 97% of Mexican children; and 96% of Cuban children. For children residing in this country for more than 10 years, the cohort of 1975-1979, the percentage who reported still speaking a native tongue other than English had not changed: 98% for Mexican, Dominican, Central American, and Cuban children; and 96% for South American youngsters.

Although all immigrant groups have shown a tendency toward bilingualism, census data indicate that Hispanic groups, more than any others, have stronger ties to their native languages. Many political, historical, and practical reasons account for this. Most Hispanics, as a supernationality, in spite of their many differences, have a common language to speak; that language unites them and gives them a sense of community. The language also helps them retain their cultural and political identity in the United States. If Asians are bound by race and Confucian values and Caribbean black immigrants are bound by color and regional identity, then most Hispanics are bound by common language. Their population size is large enough in the United States to support many Hispanic enclaves, providing sufficient job opportunities for people who speak Spanish only.

Language is an emotional and complex issue and cannot be addressed thoroughly in a few pages. Our interest here, however, is how the assimilation and language usage affect Hispanic children's educational attainment. We return to school dropout rates as the major measure to examine the effects of assimilation on attainment. Compared to other indicators, the dropout rate is a comprehensive measure of educational input, progression, and output, and we have emphasized that it is the severe dropout problem that separates Hispanics from many other groups.

Table 7.3 shows a consistent and clear trend toward a gradually declining dropout rate between the newest comers and the earlier immigrants for the total foreign-born youth at age 17 or 18. The declining curve for Mexican immigrant youth, however, is the most typical and consistent because Mexican youth are the largest number in the sample and because the social and economic characteristics of immigrants from Mexico have not varied greatly over the years by immigrant wave. Of 17-year-old Mexican children who came to the United States between 1987 and 1990, 57% are dropouts, but the percentage dropped to 27% for the 1982-1984 cohort and further dropped to 14% for the 1975-1979 cohort. The dropout rates for 18-year-olds follow the same trend. Dropout rates linked to length of U.S. residence for the other Hispanic groups also show the same trend, but less smoothly and typically. Hispanic youths are the only supernationality whose dropout rate consistently declines with increased length of U.S. residence. This pattern is less consistent for the other supernationalities.

In summary, the length of U.S. residence increases English proficiency and reduces dropout rates; but, on the other hand, the percentage of youth who speak Spanish has not declined. Along with increasing length of U.S. residence, three kinds of linguistic statuses have developed among Hispanic youth: youth who speak Spanish but do not fully develop English proficiency, youth who speak Spanish but also speak English very well, and youth who are monolingual English speakers. Taking family income into consideration, we address the question of whether these three linguistic statuses are related to the dropout rates.

Table 7.4 reveals that Mexican youth have a distinctive pattern: Those who lack English proficiency, regardless of level of family income, have the highest dropout rates—46% for low-income and 52% for high-income youth. The dropout rates for monolingual English youth, however, are twice the dropout rates of bilingual speakers: 40% for monolingual English speakers versus 21% for bilingual speakers among low-income youth, and 50% for monolingual English speakers versus 18% for bilingual speakers among high-income youth. This pattern persists among youth who dropped out with less than 5 years of education. Among youth from low-income families, 6% who lack English proficiency fall into the least educated category compared to 7% of monolingual English speakers and less than 2% of bilingual speakers. Among youth from high-income families, 7% who lack English proficiency fall

TABLE 7.3 Foreign-Born Youth Aged 5-18 Who Were Not High
School Graduates and Not Enrolled in School by Year of
Entry and Age, U.S., 1990 (in percentages)

	Age	1975-1979	1980-1981	1982-1984	1985-1986	1987-1990
Total foreign	17	8	10	11	17	31
born	18	12	17	18	30	38
White[a]	17	7	0	4	0	8
	18	3	10	0	6	5
White[b]	17	10	5	6	4	8
	18	10	7	13	10	13
Haitian	17	11	8	10	0	10
	18	0	0	6	10	14
Jamaican	17	9	10	12	12	11
	18	4	0	12	11	20
African[c]	17	10	4	19	0	8
	18	5	17	13	8	10
Mexican	17	14	16	27	43	57
	18	27	33	46	57	64
Dominican	17	15	0	5	17	25
	18	16	10	26	20	21
Cuban	17	0	6	8	15	17
	18	0	19	6	12	8
Central	17	5	13	11	13	36
American	18	14	23	22	31	49
South	17	2	7	5	6	11
American	18	8	11	10	10	19

into the least educated category compared to 10% of monolingual English speakers and less than 2% of bilingual speakers. This information challenges claims that speaking a language other than English may hamper Mexican youths' chances to graduate from high school. On the contrary, it indicates the potential danger of increasing the dropout rates if youth give up their non-English native tongues completely and become monolingual English speakers. For other Hispanic groups, this pattern occurs among all low-income youth, but only among high-income Central American youth, who show a pattern similar to that of the Mexican youth.

TABLE 7.3 Continued

	Age	1975-1979	1980-1981	1982-1984	1985-1986	1987-1990
Chinese	17	2	5	6	6	4
	18	1	5	2	6	5
Japanese	17	0	0	0	0	5
	18	0	0	0	8	3
Korean	17	8	5	2	4	2
	18	6	6	8	8	1
Asian	17	0	4	4	0	12
Indian	18	0	0	0	11	10
Filipino	17	4	8	5	0	10
	18	5	9	8	8	6
Southeast	17	2	5	8	8	12
Asian[d]	18	4	6	7	10	6

NOTE: Data from U.S. Bureau of the Census (1993b).
a. Non-Hispanic whites who came from countries where English was the dominant and official language.
b. Non-Hispanic whites who came from countries where English was not the dominant language.
c. African blacks include blacks from any country on the African continent.
d. Southeast Asian includes Cambodians, Laotians, Hmong, and Vietnamese.

Conclusions

This study supports the frequently raised concern that broad grouping of Hispanics in much research masks important variations in the social experiences of the different national origin groups who make up this heterogeneous category. Although similarities in the educational attainment of Hispanic groups can be found, important variations occur. The baseline data we report should be helpful for the development of both policy and cultural relevance in curriculum adaptation.

Sharp variations in attainment exist across national groups, and these findings, like many other studies, underscore the need to consider intraethnic variations within broadly defined groups. Mexican, Central, and Dominican Americans, for example, have lower attainment levels than other Hispanic groups and need additional educational support and intervention.

TABLE 7.4 School Dropouts by Ethnic-Nationality Group, Education Level, and Linguistic Status Among Immigrant Youth Aged 16-18, U.S. 1990 (in percentages)

	Linguistic Status	High School Dropouts[a]		Dropouts With < 5 Years' Schooling	
		Low Income	High Income	Low Income	High Income
Total foreign born	Lack proficiency[b]	30.7	31.0	4.0	4.1
	Bilingual[c]	12.0	8.2	0.7	0.6
	English only[d]	15.0	8.0	1.6	1.0
White[e]	Lack proficiency	17.5	13.6	1.6	1.0
	Bilingual	9.4	5.0	0.5	0.0
	English only	13.0	5.0	1.5	0.0
Haitian	Lack proficiency	13.0	18.0	3.0	5.0
	Bilingual	2.2	7.0	0.0	0.0
	English only	0.0	0.0	0.0	0.0
Jamaican	Lack proficiency	n.a.	n.a.	n.a.	n.a.
	Bilingual	0.0	8.0	0.0	0.0
	English only	17.0	7.0	0.0	0.0
African Black	Lack proficiency	9.0	13.0	0.0	3.7
	Bilingual	9.0	6.7	2.2	1.0
	English only	12.0	6.4	0.0	0.8
Mexican	Lack proficiency	46.3	52.0	6.2	7.2
	Bilingual	20.5	18.0	1.5	1.5
	English only	40.0	50.4	7.0	9.5
Dominican	Lack proficiency	13.0	16.0	0.0	5.0
	Bilingual	10.0	14.0	1.0	0.0
	English only	17.0	0.0	0.0	0.0
Cuban	Lack proficiency	24.0	20.0	0.0	0.0
	Bilingual	11.0	8.0	0.0	0.0
	English only	50.0	0.0	0.0	0.0
Central American	Lack proficiency	36.0	38.0	4.0	5.0
	Bilingual	11.0	9.0	0.0	1.0
	English only	37.0	42.0	16.0	17.0
South American	Lack proficiency	17.0	19.0	1.0	0.0
	Bilingual	5.0	4.0	0.0	0.0
	English only	17.0	0.0	0.0	0.0
Chinese	Lack proficiency	5.0	7.0	0.0	1.0
	Bilingual	1.0	2.0	0.0	0.0
	English only	0.0	2.0	0.0	0.0
Japanese	Lack proficiency	3.0	4.3	0.0	0.0
	Bilingual	0.0	2.0	0.0	0.0
	English only	0.0	0.0	0.0	0.0

TABLE 7.4 *Continued*

		High School Dropouts[a]		Dropouts With < 5 Years' Schooling	
	Linguistic Status	Low Income	High Income	Low Income	High Income
Korean	Lack proficiency	7.0	5.0	0.0	0.0
	Bilingual	3.0	6.0	0.0	0.0
	English only	3.0	3.0	0.0	0.0
Asian Indian	Lack proficiency	11.0	4.0	0.0	0.0
	Bilingual	0.0	2.0	0.0	0.0
	English only	0.0	1.0	0.0	0.0
Filipino	Lack proficiency	11.0	10.0	0.0	0.0
	Bilingual	9.0	5.0	0.0	0.0
	English only	0.0	4.0	0.0	0.0
Southeast Asian	Lack proficiency	11.1	7.6	0.8	1.0
	Bilingual	5.7	3.0	0.3	0.0
	English only	11.1	1.5	5.6	0.0

NOTE: Data from U.S. Bureau of the Census (1993b).

a. High school dropout: Youth who did not have a high school diploma and were not enrolled in elementary or secondary school in 1990. This may include youth who dropped out of elementary or middle school or youth who have never gone to school at any level. The majority of them dropped out of high school, however.

b. Lack proficiency: Youth who reported speaking a language other than English and cannot speak English "very well." This category includes youth who reported speaking "no English at all," "not well," and "not very well."

c. Bilingual: Youth reported speaking a language other than English and speaking English "very well."

d. English only: Youth who reported speaking no language other than English.

e. White includes only non-Hispanic whites who came from countries where English was not the dominant or official language. Among children from English language countries all of them reported speaking English very well.

Much research on educational attainment has been dominated either by an assimilationist model or a cultural ecological model. Despite variations in school enrollment and schooling attained by each nationality group and in length of U.S. residence linking to the development of English proficiency, decline of household linguistic isolation and reduction of dropout rates occur similarly across nationality groups. Our findings do not, however, fully support the assimilationist claim that more time and familiarity with U.S. culture is always better for educational success. Although the persistent gaps revealed by cross-group comparisons are consistent with Ogbu's (1978) theory, improved attainment among some cohorts does not fit the cultural ecology model. Ogbu envisions a leveling off or decline in attainment of disadvantaged caste-like minorities, such as Mexican Americans, but this study shows that significant increases in attainment occur in both political refugees (Central Americans and Southeast Asians) and caste-like minorities (Mexicans and Dominicans).

Our findings are more consistent with a cultural-contextual interactive approach (cf. Foley, 1991) that combines structural elements (e.g., forms of organization within immigrant communities, relationships of immigrants and nonimmigrants within specific locales and historical eras) and cultural elements (e.g., language, customs, values, and behavioral norms). The academic success of children of immigrants depends on acquiring some values and orientations of American culture, but avoiding full cultural assimilation into mainstream U.S. popular youth culture with its distractions that work against educational attainment. This is an additive acculturation, in which children acquire English proficiency and mainstream culture without relinquishing their traditional ways and abandoning their native languages (cf. Delgado-Gaitan, 1988; Hayes, 1992; Losey, 1995; Velez-Ibanez & Greenberg, 1992). This theory incorporates more systematic analysis of the social context of immigration for various groups at various times, including the differential responses they have received in host communities (e.g., Portes & Zhou, 1993). For example, work on educational attainment of Central American youth suggests that undocumented status (Ferris, 1987; HMP & CSUCA, 1989) and perhaps even the psychological effects of experiencing life in war-torn countries prior to immigration (Suarez-Orozco, 1989) affect attainment in the United States. More than 500,000 Central Americans fled to the United States to escape civil war, and most of them became undocumented residents (Melville, 1985). Being minority, poor, and without legal status, many Central Americans may suffer refuge symptoms and have great difficulty improving their children's education. Work on the educational and occupational status of Dominican youth also suggests that triple discrimination by race (black), ethnicity (Hispanic), and immigrant status may contribute to their lower attainment (Matthijs, 1996). These studies illustrate the problems of lumping together Hispanic groups with various backgrounds and indicate apparently segmented attainment patterns.

Educators need to reexamine traditional beliefs to consider what "Americanization" actually does to newly immigrated children of various groups. Rapid Americanization is not always beneficial for the schooling of immigrant children. When educators design programs to address the initial adjustment of immigrant children, they also need to invent strategies to help these children draw strength from their home cultures, develop a positive sense of their ethnic and immigrant identities, and nurture and maintain the native languages that can serve as resources. Carrasquillo (1991) suggests that second-language programs play a key role in the education of Hispanic students, that every bilingual program in the United States must include an English-as-a-second-language (ESL) component, and that ESL programs must recognize the importance of the mother tongue. Effective second-language programs need qualified teachers who make the classroom environment attractive to students, where they feel motivated to learn both content areas and the esecond language. If all classroom teachers were required to be bilingual, all classrooms would be multilingual environments.

Hispanic high school students are more likely than non-Hispanic white students to believe that familial well-being affects school performance, and they face formidable barriers in reconciling the characteristics of their socioeconomic and linguistic backgrounds with their educational experience. Adequate high school resources, a hospitable high school social climate, and sensitivity of high school staff to Hispanic background may be critical in optimizing Hispanic students' school achievement and preparation for college (Duran, 1983).

8

Asian
Children

How are Asian American children doing in U.S. schools? Do they
have unique social and educational needs? Should these needs be
met? Ironically, we educators know very little about this group of students
too often dismissed as the "model minority." Asian immigration to the
United States has expanded dramatically in the past two decades. Although Asian Americans have more than 150 years' history of immigration to this country, about 90% of Asian Americans are recent immigrants and their U.S.-born children who arrived since the 1965
Immigration Act. The number of emigrants from Asian countries has
risen rapidly since then, and the Asian American population has doubled in each of the past three decades: 1.7 million in 1970, 3 million in
1980, 6.8 million in 1990, about 10 million in 1995, and possibly 17.1
million in 2010.

In this chapter we first use the recent census data to examine a number of assumptions about Asian American children: their family income
and family type, their numbers and length of U.S. residence, and their
language resources. These data are cross-tabulated by the major Asian
nationalities of the immigrants. We compare current census data
against historical data to identify the new features of recent Asian immigrants and to examine the reported inter-intra group polarization:
On one hand, people with rich "ethnic-class cultural and economic re-

sources"; on the other, a permanent underclass stagnating in ethnic neighborhoods, speaking no English, and having little education.

The educational attainment of Asian immigrant children is presented in two sections: first, school enrollment and school completion at various levels of education, including acceleration rates and school dropout rates; second, educational attainment, language use, and adaptation, indicating the relationship among schooling, linguistic adaptation, and length of U.S. residence.

Finally, we address issues for Asian students being the model minority through discussion of "cross-overs," "double minority," and "marginal minority" from Asian Americans' perspectives. This section outlines the special needs of Asian immigrant children and offers recommendations for educators, policymakers, and parents. This section also suggests lessons educators can draw from their experience working with Asian immigrant children and whether these lessons apply to educating other immigrant children.

Socioeconomic Profile and Language Resources of Asian Immigrant Children

Our sources of information for this section are data we compiled from the 1990 census, *We the Asian Americans* (Paisano, 1993), and other publications of the U.S. Bureau of the Census. The 1990 census counted 7 million Asians, about a 100% increase over the 1980 census count. The largest proportions of Asians were Chinese (24%), Filipino (20%), Japanese (12.3%), Asian Indian (11.8%), Korean (11.6%), and Vietnamese (9%). Hmong, Cambodian, and Laotian peoples together account for less than 6% of the Asian population. Two of three U.S. Asians were born in foreign countries. Vietnamese, Laotian, and Cambodian groups had the highest proportion of Asian foreign born, whereas Japanese had the lowest proportion. Two of five Asians entered the United States between 1980 and 1990. Three quarters of Vietnamese, Cambodians, Laotians, and Hmong have entered this country since 1975. The Hmong and Cambodians, with their large proportions of recent immigrants, were the youngest Asians with a median age of 13 and 19, respectively. They have higher fertility rates and larger families than both other Asian groups and the native-born population. Among Asian groups,

Hmong had the largest family size with 6.6 persons, and Japanese the smallest family size with 3.1 persons.

In 1990, 78% of all Asians 25-years-old and older were high school graduates; the national rate was 75%.

Education is highly valued in Asian communities, but the educational attainment of different groups varies widely. The proportion completing high school or higher was 88% for Japanese, compared with 31% for Hmong. This also differs by gender: Asian adult men had higher rates of high school graduation than Asian women—82% versus 74% in 1990. Of Japanese women, 86% had a high school diploma compared with 19% for Hmong women. At the college level, 38% of Asians had graduated with a bachelor's degree or higher by 1990, compared with 20% of the total population. Asian Indian males had the highest attainment rates (66%), and Cambodians, Laotians, and Hmong had the lowest (3%). The next lowest percentage of college degrees is Vietnamese (17%).

Asian families had higher median family incomes ($41,583) in 1989 than all families ($35,255), because of more family members in the workforce and higher educational attainment. About 11% of Asian families were living in poverty in 1989, a rate slightly higher than the 10% for all American families. Hmong and Cambodian families had the highest family poverty rates, 62% and 42%, respectively. The poverty rate for Vietnamese was 26%. The lowest poverty rates were for Filipino (5%) and Japanese (3%) families. Asians were more likely than the total population to have jobs in technical, sales, and administrative support and managerial and professional specialties, but the proportion in technical, sales, and administrative support occupations varies from 37% of Korean workers to 5% of Laotian workers. Fifty-four percent of the Asian population lived in the West in 1990, and approximately 66% of Asians lived in just five states—California, New York, Hawaii, Texas, and Illinois (Paisano, 1993).

According to census data, about 76% of 5- to 18-year-old U.S. children who live with parents were living with both parents in 1990. That year, 82% of Asian immigrant children were living with their parents: 93% of Japanese children, 92% of Indian children, 85% of Korean children, 83% of Chinese children, and 76% of Southeast Asian children. These percentages are significantly higher than the percentage for the total foreign-born children (75%) and also higher than most ethnic and nationality groups. It is lower only than non-Hispanic white children from English language countries (85%). Although the proportion of Asian female-headed families was significantly less than the national average, 12% versus 17%, Cambodians had proportions above the national average—26%.

Most foreign-born Asian children come from recently immigrated families with lower incomes than native-born Asian families, but with higher average family income levels compared to the total U.S. population. The income of long-time U.S. residents who were foreign-born Asians, however, was higher than that of native Asian families. Among the eight subsupernationality groups—non-Hispanic whites from English language countries, non-Hispanic whites from non-English language countries, Caribbean blacks, African blacks, Mexicans, Hispanics other than Mexicans, Southeast Asians, and Asians other than Southeast Asians—the family income of Asian immigrant children is lower only than that of non-Hispanic white immigrants from English language countries. It is significantly higher than all Hispanic and black groups. Even so, the average family income of Southeast Asians is significantly lower than that of the total immigrant children, all other Asian groups, all black groups, and all Hispanic groups except Mexicans and Dominicans. Southeast Asian children are also more likely than most groups except Mexicans and Dominicans to be living in poverty. Among Asian immigrant children, Chinese and Korean children came from families with lower incomes and with higher poverty levels than Japanese children, whose families have the highest income among all 15 groups including non-Hispanic whites from English language countries. Chinese and Korean families also have lower income than Filipino families and Asian Indian families.

The lower family income and poverty among Southeast Asian families, compared to other Asian immigrant children, cannot be explained by shortness of U.S. residence, because the largest cohort of Southeast Asians arrived in the United States before 1985. Eighty percent of Japanese children and 50% of Koreans, Chinese, and Filipinos had arrived in this country within the past 5 years, whereas only 37% of Southeast Asian children had arrived since 1985. Sixty-seven percent of Japanese children and about 30% of Chinese, Korean, and Filipino children had arrived in the United States less than 3 years prior to the 1990 census.

Low family income and poverty may be explained, however, by variations within the group. A distinctive gap occurs in the demographic and socioeconomic characteristics between Vietnamese and Hmong, Cambodian, and Laotian groups; a gap also occurs between Southeast Asians and other Asian groups in conditions before and during immigration (war and political refugees) and in being largely first-generation immigrants. Unlike East Asians and Filipinos, who have a history of immigration to the United States that extends over 100 years and more than five generations, 95% of Southeast Asians are foreign-born and therefore do not have the ethnic communities, ethnic industries, and employment networks of longer term and better established U.S. residents (cf. Smith-Hefner, 1990, 1993).

Almost all Asian children spoke a native tongue other than English shortly after they arrived in the United States (95%). English is, however, the official language in India, the Philippines, and Hong Kong; therefore, children from these areas may speak better English than other Asian children and may be more likely to become English-only speakers than other children. Among the most recent cohort arriving between 1987 and 1990, 20% of Indian and 8% of Filipino children reported themselves as English-only speakers, compared to 2% of Chinese and Southeast Asians and 3% of Japanese and Koreans. Filipinos also reported the highest percentage (50%) of children with English proficiency, followed by Indian children (42%), Koreans (23%), Chinese (21%), Japanese (18%), and Southeast Asians (11%). Among the 180,000 Southeast Asian immigrant children for whom English was not the primary language, the most-used languages were Vietnamese (90,000), Mon-Khmer (40,000), and Thai (30,000).

Income seems to have a significant impact on Asian children's English proficiency. Among the children who spoke a native tongue other than English, children from families of higher income were more likely to report speaking English very well than children from lower-income families. This pattern persists even after controlling for the year of entry and is true for both Southeast Asians and other Asians (see Table 3.1, this volume). Among the most recent cohort, 21% of Asian immigrant children and 11% of Southeast Asians who came from low-income families reported speaking English very well, compared to 34% and 15% from high-income families, respectively. Among the 1975-1979 cohort, 82% of Asian immigrant children and 78% of Southeast Asians who came from high-income families reported speaking English very well, compared to 78% and 63% from low-income families, respectively.

The Educational Attainment
of Asian Immigrant Children

Despite the long history of major Asian groups in the United States, they remain a first-generation immigrant population. Immigrant children far outnumber native-born Asian American children. Their cultures are radically different from U.S. culture, and they have a viable and solid ethnic community and distinct racial features. Asian Americans have suffered severe persecution and discrimination, yet they have maintained a hold on their own cultures for more than a century in the United States (Sung, 1987). Asian children as a whole have the most schooling, the highest grade-point averages, the lowest dropout rates, and an overrepresentation in the gifted programs in almost all states across the United States (U.S. Department of Education, 1993a, 1993b). Even when controlling for socioeconomic difference, Asian children's performance patterns persist.

Previous research with cross-racial and ethnic group comparisons shows that Asian students generally have done better than either black or Hispanic students in school and equally well or slightly better than non-Hispanic white students in years of school completed, percentage of high school graduates, percentage of college graduates, and most other educational measures (Rong & Grant, 1992). This fits evidence we have discussed already that immigrant minorities persist in school longer and, once initial language handicaps are overcome, achieve a greater degree of academic success than nonimmigrant involuntary racial minorities (Gibson, 1988; Ogbu, 1987). Although Asian Americans currently constitute only 3% of students in U.S. schools, their educational attainment is instructive to study. Their dual status of being minority and immigrant causes some researchers to anticipate such youths may be less successful in U.S. schools. Others consider these immigrants to be a "minority success story" (Suzuki, 1977).

Enrollment and School Completion

School enrollment rates among Asian immigrants aged 6-16 are higher than the average enrollment rates for foreign-born children as a whole, and also higher than all other groups except non-Hispanic whites from English language countries. Minor variation occurs among the six Asian groups: 3% of Japanese, Chinese, and Asian Indian children were not in school, compared to 5% of Korean, Filipino, and Southeast Asian children.

Asian immigrant children have one of the highest elementary school and middle school completion rates compared to the total native-born children and the total foreign-born children and one of the highest high school completion rates among youth aged 18—equal to the total native-born youth and higher than the average rate for the total foreign-born population. Asian immigrant children generally do well in U.S. schools in school completion, compared to immigrants of other ethnic and nationality groups in the United States. Among children aged 12-18, about 99% of Chinese, Korean, and Asian Indian children; 98% of Japanese and Filipino children; and 97% of Southeast Asian children had finished elementary school in 1990 (see Table 7.1, this volume). Among children aged 14-18, 81% of Korean; 79% of Japanese; 78% of Chinese, Asian Indian, and Filipino; and 73% of Southeast Asian children had completed 8 years of schooling. The high school graduation rates for most Asian groups at age 18 are adequate except for Southeast Asians. It may, however, take more years for these children to finish high school than other children. The dropout rates for all Asian groups are low.

Education, Linguistic Status, and Adaptation

For all Asian groups, length of U.S. residence significantly promotes English proficiency, although each at a different pace. In 1990, among the cohort who came to the United States between 1987 and 1990, 62% of Asian Indians, 57% of Filipinos, 26% of Koreans, 20% of Chinese, 20% of Japanese, and 12% of Southeast Asians reported spoken English proficiency. The percentages increase dramatically for the cohort who arrived between 1975 and 1979—90% of Koreans, Asian Indians, and Filipinos; 80% of Chinese; 74% of Japanese; and 72% of Southeast Asians reported proficiency in speaking English. Among all Asians, Southeast Asian immigrant youth by far show the largest scale of improvement (600%) in their English proficiency between the 1987 cohort and 1975 cohort.

The percentage of children living in linguistically isolated households has also steadily and significantly declined, along with increasing length of U.S. residency for all Asian groups. Among the cohort who came to the United States between 1987 and 1990, 20% of Asian Indians and Filipinos; 65% of Chinese, Japanese, and Koreans; and 73% of Southeast Asians lived in a linguistically isolated household in 1990. For the cohort who came to this country between 1975 and 1979, only 4% of Filipino, 8% of Asian Indian, 11% of Korean, 19% of Chinese, and 23% of Japanese immigrant children were still living in linguistically isolated household in 1990.

Like the trend for Hispanic groups, 10 years of U.S. residence bring Asian children more English language usage adaptation. Similar to Hispanic groups, this tendency is toward bilingualism. Almost all Asian immigrant children who came to the United States between 1987 and 1990 reported speaking an Asian language at home (100% of Southeast Asians; 98% of Chinese, Koreans, and Japanese; 92% of Filipinos; and 80% of Asian Indians). For most Asian children who had resided in this country for more than 10 years, the cohort of 1975-1979, the percentage who reported still speaking a language other than English changed very little: 95% for Southeast Asians; 92% for Chinese, 82% for Japanese and Koreans; and 73% for Asian Indians. Filipinos at 43% were an exception.

Although all immigrant groups from non-English language countries have shown a tendency toward bilingualism, census data reveal that Asian groups have weaker ties to their native languages than do Hispanics. Some Asian groups, such as Filipinos who came from countries where English is an official language, show a trend toward English monolingualism. Rong (1997) reports that among second-generation Asians, more than 95% reported speaking English very well, and the proportion of children who reported speaking a language other than English dropped to less than 20%. Among the third generation, all reported speaking English very well, and the percentage of children who reported speaking a language other than English at home decreased to less than 5%. Although researchers report great efforts made within Asian American communities to retain their language and their cultural heritage, this may be a difficult aspiration. Without a unified language spoken among all Asians, retention of native tongues may be more difficult for Asians than for Hispanics. More than 50 languages are spoken by Asian immigrants, and many languages and dialects are also spoken within one nationality category such as Chinese. Asians have not been bound by language, and the cultural symbol of their supernationality is not represented by native tongues, although native languages may be the cultural symbol for each nationality. Other factors, such as culture, religion, written characters, philosophy, and family and personal values, have been shared among many, if not all, Asian groups. For example, Chinese characters have been retained in Japanese and Korean calligraphy. Confucian thought on education, family values, and the relationship between authority and the individual have been honored in East, Southeast, and South Asia for many centuries. Buddhism and its versions have also been adopted among people in almost every country on the Asian continent.

How does language transition affect children's educational attainment? How do the effects differ across groups? Again, we use school dropout rates as the measure to study the effects of assimilation on attainment. No clear pattern emerges on how the length of U.S. residence affects the dropout rates among Asian immigrant children of various groups. Southeast Asian 17-year-olds are the only group with a pattern similar to Mexican immigrant children (see Table 7.3, this volume). Of 17-year-old Southeast Asian children who came to the United States between 1987 and 1990, 12% are dropouts; the percentage dropped to 8% for the 1982-1984 cohort and further dropped to 2% for the 1975-1979 cohort. The dropout rates for 18-year-olds seem to follow the same trend except for the 1987-1990 cohort. Of all Asian groups, Southeast Asian youths are the only subsupernationality with this trend—a decline in dropping out with increased length of U.S. residence. In many cases, youth in the current cohort are less likely to drop out of school than the earlier cohort.

Finally, does the combined effects of length of U.S. residence, linguistic adaptation, and family income affect Asian children's dropout rates? We divided immigrant children by three linguistic statuses: youth who speak an Asian language, but lack English proficiency; youth who speak an Asian language but also speak English very well; and youth who are monolingual English speakers. Our data disclose a general pattern: Asian youth who lack English proficiency, regardless of level of family income, have the highest dropout rates (see Table 7.4, this volume). Among youth from high-income families, however, the dropout rates for youth who were monolingual English speakers were lower than the dropout rates of the bilingual speakers for most of the Asian groups. Among youth from low-income families, no clear pattern differentiates the effect of English monolingualism or bilingualism on dropping out. Youth from low-income families who are bilingual speakers do not necessarily drop out of school at higher rates than the monolingual English speakers, except for Filipino children—0 versus 9% in favor of monolingual English speakers. Southeast Asians show a pattern similar to Mexicans: Monolingual English speakers were more likely to drop out of school than bilingual speakers—11% of monolingual English speakers versus 6% of bilingual speakers.

Asians generally have very low dropout rates, and few Asian dropouts fall into the category of the least educated—less than 5 years of schooling. Dropouts from low-income families in the Southeast Asian group are more frequently monolingual English speakers (6%) than bilingual speakers with and without English proficiency.

Our findings on Asian Americans contradict the common image of Southeast Asian immigrants (cf. Caplan, Choy, & Whitmore, 1991; Trueba, Jacobs, & Kirton, 1990). Because of their low-socioeconomic status and their difficulties before and during immigration, Southeast Asian immigrant children have been predicted to have substantial problems in educational attainment. The 1990 census data reveal, however, that these children actually did better than children in most other groups at socioeconomic levels similar to theirs (e.g., Central American children) or better than groups at socioeconomic levels higher than theirs (e.g., some black and Hispanic groups). Southeast Asian children have lagged behind other Asian children partially because of their particular situations. Nevertheless, the differences in educational attainment for Asian children aged 5-18 do not reflect the bipolar trend found among adult Asians in parental education, family income, and immigration condition.

Conclusions

What we have shown here is that no one factor is accountable for immigrant children's schooling; outcomes are produced through the interaction of factors at various levels and dimensions (cf. Lee, 1994). Our findings agree more with a selective assimilation model than either the classic assimilation model or the cultural production-reproduction model. Positive effects of assimilation are reflected in improvement in English proficiency with increasing length of U.S. residence and in reduction of dropout rates among youth who have developed oral English proficiency. Fluctuation in dropout rates across cohorts contradicts what is generally believed, however: Longer residence in the United States increases exposure to English and familiarity with schools and other social institutions, which in turn may lead to higher attainment. Furthermore, some more recently immigrated Asians have lower dropout rates than long-time residents, and among Southeast Asian children from low-income families, the bilingual speakers have significantly lower dropout rates than monolingual English speakers. Classical assimilation theory also fails to explain the persistent educational gap between Southeast Asians and the other five Asian groups.

Selective assimilation theory explains variation in educational attainment among different cohorts as a result of increased acculturation of students to youth popular culture and increased adaptations to student oppositional cultures. The different educational attainment patterns across the six Asian groups may also reflect the effects of different structural conditions the various groups encounter: factors relating to country of origin and receptivity in the new country, such as attitudes of local community residents and governmental policies at various levels; availability of resources in the United States and the home country; internal differentiation within the group by age and sex; spatial concentration; and the length of time others from the group have resided in the United States. Of all Asian groups (Zhou & Bankston, 1994), Southeast Asians, by most accounts, suffer the worst discrimination and face more barriers in multiethnic schools. For some Southeast Asian youths, unlike most others, longer U.S. residence may engender more, rather than less, discrimination as they become incorporated into an indigenous minority group highly stigmatized and oppressed by the dominant groups. The higher dropout rates among monolingual English-speaking children of Southeast Asian immigrants can be explained as overassimilation or assimilation into an oppositional culture.

Kuo (1982) has found that some immigrant Chinese, highly trained and more successful in their professions as a group than American-born Chinese, were structurally assimilated but not always culturally assimilated. They have kept close ties with kin in their home countries through international phone calls, Internet activity, and frequent international air travel. They celebrate traditional festivals and drink tea and wines in an "exotic" way. They speak their mother tongues with no apology and send their children to Chinese Sunday language schools to maintain the home language, culture, and values. The 40 finalists of the prestigious Westinghouse award over the past 10 years have included many of the sons and daughters of these Chinese professionals. In contrast, other immigrant youth who have resided in the United States long enough to become monolingual English speakers may have fully assimilated into the dysfunctional patterns associated with some responses to poverty—this pattern has been common among our Mexican and some Southeast Asian newcomers.

The success of Asian Americans in recent years serves to illustrate the effects of broad social factors on what happens to immigrants. Lee and Rong (1988) explain Asian success through the interaction of a favorable social-political environment with relevant cultural attributes and key demographic characteristics. Using historical data, they show that Asian Americans have not always done well. On arriving in the United States in 1849, the Chinese were viewed by many native-born Americans as being inferior and incapable of intellectual development. They were banned from educational and business opportunities. No progress was made for a long time. After more than a century of difficulty in the United States, the same group has been recently praised as the model minority, and Asian successes are explained by some scholars as resulting from high intelligence and cultural fitness (e.g., Herrnstein & Murray, 1994). Our belief is that Asian success in the United States has been a function of historical timing. In the era of the emergent Pacific Rim, a match has occurred between the experiences and skills of Asian immigrants, on one hand, and societal needs and opportunity structures, on the other (cf. Kim, 1993). As U.S. markets have become dependent on international trade with Asian countries, foreign investment, and imported engineers and scientists, expanding Japanese investment and the influx of Asian professionals and business people have met these changed needs.

Most Asian children are doing well in school, but this does not mean that U.S. schools are doing well by Asian children or that Asian parents are satisfied with the schools their children attend. In addition to concerns about the quality of education schools provide and the discipline problems in many middle and high schools, parents have other issues. First, recruitment of Asian American teachers is crucial to improving the quality of education Asian American children receive. Only 1% of the nation's elementary and secondary schoolteachers were Asian in 1990, but Asian students accounted for more than 3% of the U.S. elementary and secondary student population (Rong & Preissle, 1997). Asian youth may need more help from their teachers than the native born, because two of three Asians are foreign born, and many of them have linguistic and cultural problems. They may also suffer racial discrimination and economic barriers with no understanding of what is happening because these may be new experiences for them.

The nation's schools have been particularly unprepared for Southeast Asian students. To help this group, the Center for Applied Linguistics (CAL) reprinted Vietnamese school textbooks in English so that teachers could learn more about what their new students had studied. But sometimes no previous study had occurred. In the mid-1980s, teacher groups consulted by CAL reported difficulties with an increasing number of refugee children who had virtually no education because they had been in transit as refugees for as long as 10 years. Teenagers from Laos and Cambodia were particularly at risk in the schools on this account. The same condition is currently being reported for many new arrivals from Central America, where youngsters have often bypassed educational systems altogether (Stewart, 1993).

Asian parents and students alike want to modify the current school curricula to reflect a more multicultural approach. Asian children from non-Western cultures who are asked to study only European values and history may perceive that their own cultural heritage is unimportant or inferior. Sung (1987) reports that many Asian youth whom she interviewed complained that they live in the projected image of the host country with no Asian "character model" or "media model" in popular culture. Secondary schools should develop courses on the history of Asian countries and of Asian American immigration to the United States. Schools also need to develop Asian American minority studies to increase students' awareness of the problems and difficulties Asian Americans are facing today.

Asian educational issues have received little attention among policymakers, because youth in this group have been assumed to be doing well, compared with other minority groups. Census data do, however, show considerable variations in high school completion rates and dropout rates among Asian youth. Southeast Asian immigrant youth are hampered by their lack of English proficiency and other personal and family characteristics. Asian immigrant youth from non-English-speaking and low-socioeconomic backgrounds have been retained in school and have dropped out because their language needs were not met. Attention to these patterns is crucial because Asian immigrants have the highest percentage of youth coming to the United States at older ages. Ignoring these youngsters' urgent needs because other members of the same ethnic group are doing relatively well in U.S. schools is not a sound policy (Hsia, 1988; Peng & Wright, 1994; Wei, 1986).

9

Caribbean and African Black Children

" No one wants us." This is the sentiment of Haitian Americans, explaining why U.S. immigration policy on Haiti's boat people has been "sending them all back." It reflects the current situation of black immigrants in the United States and explains why their numbers historically have been suppressed and their special needs neglected.

Hostility and discrimination against black people in the United States have been historically strong and deep. The black population has the smallest proportion of post-1900 immigrants of all racial and ethnic groups in the United States. As we have already noted, almost the entire black population of the United States is descended from slaves brought forcibly to the New World before the middle of the 19th century. Conflicts of interest have developed between African Americans and immigrants, sometimes between long-time residents and fresh newcomers of the same race. Blacks usually coexist with immigrant minorities in urban areas. Many blacks believe that their share of the national and local social services budgets has decreased because newly immigrated minority people require the same services. Leaders of African American communities have found themselves at odds with immigrants over how scarce education dollars should be spent. Competition has developed for low-paying work and service jobs. Furthermore, recent black immigrants who came to the United States voluntarily are qualified for an affirmative action originally designed to help African Americans by eliminating discrimination and segregation in education and employment (Stewart, 1993).

Without strong domestic advocacy most likely to come from people of the same racial or ethnic group (e.g., Cuban Americans advocating for Cuban refugees, Irish Americans adding the underrepresented Irish as a new category to the immigration quota), the number of black immigrants from Africa has been kept very low. Black immigrants from Haiti, Jamaica, and Africa together account for less than 5% of immigrants in 1994. The number is rising, however. With the increased numbers in the public schools, educators must be prepared to meet the educational needs of these children—needs different from those of the domestic black population.

Census data (U.S. Bureau of the Census, 1983b) indicate that in 1960 less than 125,000 foreign-born black people lived in the United States. The number surged to 1,596,000 by 1994 (Hansen & Bachu, 1995), almost double the 1980 population (815,000). As the immigrant black population has grown, its proportion of the foreign-born population has also increased: The foreign born constituted 0.7% of the U.S. black population in 1960, 1.1% in 1970, 3% in 1980, and about 5% in 1994. Census projections show that the foreign-born population among blacks will double in 20 years from 1.6 million in 1990 to 2.7 million in 2010, and the proportion of the foreign born in the black population will increase from 4.6% to 7.3%.

Non-Hispanic Caribbeans (mostly Grenadine, Haitian, Jamaican, Trinidadian, and Tobagoian) and Africans (mostly Ethiopian, Ghanaian, Nigerian, and South African) make up the majority of the 1.6 million foreign-born people of African origin in the 1990s. Immigration to the United States from Caribbean islands has been small throughout the 20th century, but its numbers significantly grew following the change in the immigration law in 1965 (Kasinitz, 1992). For example, well over half of the legal immigrants from Haiti to the United States entered after 1968, in addition to the large influx of undocumented Haitian immigrants of the 1980s. According to 1990 census data (U.S. Bureau of the Census, 1993a), approximately 230,000 Haitians and 334,000 Jamaicans compose the majority of non-Hispanic Caribbean blacks. Matthijs (1996) reports that Caribbean blacks are heavily overrepresented in the Northeast and concentrated in a few states. About half of them live in New York, 17% in Florida, 7% in New Jersey, and 4% in Massachusetts. Virtually all of them live in large cities, primarily New York and Miami. Compared to the Caribbean immigrant population, the number of foreign-born blacks from each of the African countries is small and distributed relatively evenly. Nigeria has contributed the largest number to the foreign-born population from African nations, but its 55,000 is much smaller than newcomers from either Haiti or Jamaica. Consequently, no large ethnic communities for black African immigrants are found in the United States.

Sociodemographic Profile and Linguistic Status

Haitian, Jamaican, and African, the three largest groups, compose the majority of black immigrant children in the United States. Among the 110,000 black immigrant children, 19,000 came from Haiti, 30,000 from Jamaica, and about 21,000 from the African continent. Among children from Africa, Ethiopia (4,000), Nigeria (3,000), South Africa (2,700), and Central Africa (5,000) are the top four major contributors to the population.

According to census data, less than 40% of native-born black children who live with parents were living with both parents in 1990. The percentage of black immigrant children who lived with both parents was much higher than that of native-born blacks. In 1990, 58% of black immigrant children were living with their parents, 56% of Haitian children, and 59% of Jamaican and African children. These percentages are lower than those for all foreign-born children (76%) and for most ethnic and nationality groups. Only Dominican children have a lower percentage (50%) living with both parents than black immigrant children.

Foreign-born black children come mainly from recent immigrant families with incomes lower than native-born black families and lower than the average U.S. family income. The income level of long-time U.S. foreign-born residents, however, was similar to that of native black families. Among the foreign-born population, the family income of black immigrant children is lower only than that of white immigrant children and some of the Asian groups; it is significantly higher than most Hispanic and Southeast Asian groups. Less poverty is found among Jamaican and African children than among all major Hispanic groups and Southeast Asians. Among black immigrant children, Haitian children came from families with the lowest income and with the highest poverty level, and

Jamaican children came from families with the highest income and lowest poverty level.

The lower family income and higher poverty level among Haitian families, compared to other black immigrant children, can be partially explained by their more recent immigration than the other two groups. Fifty-one percent of Jamaican children, 54% of African children, but 63% of Haitian children had arrived in this country within 5 years of 1990, including 42% of Haitian children who had been in the United States less than 3 years.

Almost all Jamaican children spoke English before their emigration, and two of three African immigrant children came from families in which English was the primary language. Only one in 10 Haitian immigrant children used English, their primary languages being French and French Creole. Among the 7,000 African immigrant children for whom English was not the primary language, the most-used language was French Creole, followed by French, Amharic, Nigerian, and Spanish.

Income seems to have no significant impact on black children's English proficiency. Among the children who spoke a native tongue other than English, 45% of Haitian immigrant children who came from low-income families reported speaking English very well, compared to 49% from higher-income families. This pattern persists even after controlling for the year of entry.

The Educational Attainment of Black Immigrant Children

Previous research with cross-racial and ethnic group comparisons has shown that domestic black students do less well than either white or Asian students in school, but better than Mexican and Puerto Rican students in years of school completed, percentage of high school graduates, percentage of college graduates, and most other educational measures (e.g., Arias, 1986; Grant & Rong, 1996; Matute-Bianchi, 1986). Studies on the schooling of black immigrant children are scarce, however.

Although black immigrants may currently constitute a small percentage of students in U.S. schools, their dual status of black and immigrant especially interests sociological researchers. Although some anticipated they would be less successful in U.S. schools because they faced the double barriers of xenophobia and racism, others have regarded them as a "black success story" in a racially segregated society (Butcher, 1994; Farley & Walter, 1989; Model, 1991). This fits the increasing evidence we have noted that immigrant minorities persist in school longer and, once initial language handicaps are overcome, achieve more academic success than nonimmigrant involuntary minorities (Gibson & Bhachu, 1991; Ogbu, 1978, 1987).

Immigration, Education, and Identity

Studies hypothesizing about different levels of motivation and work ethic among Caribbean and African immigrants have focused on differences between modern American and Caribbean society (e.g., Wilson, 1987). Matthijs (1996) observes that although many American blacks have entered the middle class in recent decades, structural changes in U.S. society, such as the deterioration of manufacturing and the flight of the middle class to the suburbs, have deprived many young urban blacks of successful models for achievement in their communities. Most Caribbean immigrant blacks face similar problems, but blacks have traditionally composed the majority in the Caribbean islands and have occupied a more diverse range of positions in the social hierarchy. The past experiences of more positive examples of black achievement and less rigid social classification of racial groups in these societies may lead to a stronger orientation toward socioeconomic achievement among Caribbean immigrant blacks and to their different responses to race issues in the United States.

For immigrants, becoming U.S. citizens necessitates developing a knowledge and perception of racism and its effects and subtle nuances because large differences occur in white and minority Americans' perceptions and expectations of the world. In her ethnographic study of Caribbean blacks, Waters (1991, 1994) reports that several identities are evident among these immigrant youths: an immigrant identity associated with nationality such as Haitian and Jamaican, a pan-national identity such as Caribbean or West Indian, a pan-racial identity such as black American, and an unhyphenated American identity. Although foreign-born black youths are more likely to choose a national-origin identity, the length of U.S. residence of their families may shift their preference to a pan-national identity or a pan-ethnic identity.

These identity studies (e.g., Foner, 1987; Kasinitz, 1992; Stafford, 1987; Waters, 1991, 1994; Woldemikael, 1989) help explain how black students' educational attainment has varied by their immigrant generational status. According to Waters (1994), different identities are related to different perceptions and understandings of race relations and opportunities in the United States, and produce different results in school. Youngsters who identify as ethnic Caribbean blacks see more opportunities and rewards for their individual efforts and initiative, work longer hours, and watch less television. Youngsters who identify as black Americans focus more on the racial discrimination that limits opportunities for blacks in the United States. They also are more likely to associate with oppositional cultures. Therefore, they have tended to do less well in school.

Waters (1994) also reports factors influencing the type of identity the youngsters have developed. These include the social class background of the parents, parents' social networks, the type of school the child attends, and family structure and parental authority.

To simplify subsequent text, we refer to the three major groups of immigrant Americans in this chapter by nationality, Haitian blacks and Jamaican blacks, and pan-nationality, African blacks, those who have migrated directly from Africa to the United States. We use the reference category white for non-Hispanic white Americans. The educational attainment of black immigrant children is discussed in two sections. The first focuses on school enrollment and school completion at various levels of education, including acceleration rates and school dropout rates. Attainment, language, and adaptation, the second section, examines the relationship among schooling, linguistic adaptation, and length of U.S. residence.

Enrollment and School Completion

School enrollment rates among black immigrants 6 to 16 years old are equal to or higher than the average enrollment rates for foreign-born children as a whole and are higher than all Hispanic groups except South Americans. Little variation occurs among the three black groups: 6% of African children were not in school, compared to 7% of Jamaican and Haitian children.

Black immigrant children have higher elementary school and middle school completion rates than the average rates for native-born children and foreign-born children (see Table 7.1, this volume); high school completion rates among youth aged 18 are equal to native-born youth and higher than the average rate for the foreign-born population. Black immigrant children generally did well in U.S. schools in school completion, compared to immigrants of most ethnic and nationality groups.

Black immigrant youth tend to stay in school until receiving their high school diplomas. At age 17, 93% of Haitian, and 90% of Jamaican and African youth either graduated or still were in school, compared to 91% nationwide for native-born youth, and 82% for total foreign-born youth. At age 18, 92% of Haitian, 88% of Jamaican, and 89% of African immigrant youth were still in school, compared to 88% nationwide for all native-born youth, and 74% for all foreign-born youth (see Table 7.2, this volume). Among these youth who are school dropouts, few are truly undereducated—with less than 5 years of schooling.

The census data thus present a positive picture of black immigrant children's education. Better yet is that black immigrant children are more likely to be ahead of others in grade levels. Table 9.1 indicates that at age 10, only 19% of native-born children and 26% of foreign-born children had finished 5 years of elementary school in 1990. Among black immigrant children, however, 30% of Jamaicans and Africans had completed elementary school. At age 14, 17% of native-born children and 21% of foreign-born children had finished 8 years of school in 1990, compared to 26% of Haitian, 23% of Jamaican, and 31% of African immigrant children. At age 17, 11% of Haitian, 16% of Jamaican, and 17% of African immigrant children had graduated from high school, compared to 6% of native-born children and 8% of foreign-born children. The 17% high school completion rate among 17-year-old African black youth was the highest for any group including non-Hispanic whites from English language countries.

These rates may reflect the higher percentage of black immigrant children who go to school at an early age, stay in school, and make satisfactory academic progress. This is one aspect of the polarization of education among most immigrant groups. Immigrant children are more likely than the native born to begin school later, such as age 7 or 8, move through school more slowly, and drop out of school at all levels of education. Some of them are, however, also more likely to enter school earlier and maintain a faster pace than native-born children.

Education, Language, and Adaptation

The adaptation of black immigrant children in the United States and how it is related to their educational attainment may help educators better understand the debates over assimilation, acculturation, and multiculturalism in immigrant children's schooling. This may also suggest implications of and applications for related educational policy.

TABLE 9.1 Acceleration Rates at Various Levels of Education, by Ethnicity and Age, U.S., 1990 (in percentages)

	Elementary (5 Year) Age 10	Middle (8 Year) Age 14	Secondary (12 Year) Age 17
Total native born	19	17	6
Total foreign born	26	21	8
White[a]	27	15	13
White[b]	28	23	14
Haitian	24	26	11
Jamaican	30	23	16
African[c]	30	31	17
Mexican	26	19	7
Dominican	33	26	13
Cuban	27	24	6
Central American	24	21	5
South American	29	32	11
Chinese	30	25	8
Japanese	12	8	2
Korean	25	22	6
Asian Indian	36	23	14
Filipino	25	18	14
Southeast Asian[d]	19	16	6

NOTE: Data from U.S. Bureau of the Census (1993b).
a. Non-Hispanic whites who came from countries where English was the dominant and official language.
b. Non-Hispanic whites who came from countries where English was not the dominant language.
c. African blacks include blacks from any country on the African continent.
d. Southeast Asian includes Cambodians, Laotians, Hmong, and Vietnamese.

We first conduct comparisons among the most recent immigrants, the ones who arrived in the United States between 1987 and 1990, with the ones who arrived between 1975 and 1979. Findings in Table 7.3 (this volume) reveal a national trend supporting the classical assimilation theory—the longer children reside in the United States, the better they do in school. This is true for 17-year-olds: The dropout rate falls gradually from 31% for the 1987-1990 cohort to 8% for the 1975-1979 cohort. It is also true for 18-year-olds. But, the dropout rate change is different for various groups, and the general pattern does not hold for these three black immigrant groups. Among black immigrant children, the length of U.S. residence does not necessarily reduce the dropout rates. For some earlier cohorts, the rates increase. At best, the data supporting traditional assimilation theory for black immigrant children's schooling are inconsistent and inconclusive.

Census data also reveal how length of U.S. residence rapidly affects language. Immigrant children who have resided in the United States for 10 or more years are more likely to develop English proficiency, less likely to live in a linguistically isolated household, but may not have given up their native tongues. Haitian children serve as an example of this; the majority are relatively recent immigrants, and more than 90% come from homes in which English is not the primary language. Data on Haitian children show that linguistic adjustment tends toward bilingualism. Among the most recent Haitian immigrant children, 4 of 10 reported having spoken English proficiency. This figure increases to almost 9 of 10 for those living in the United States 10 or more years. Among Haitian children from the 1987-1990 cohort who speak a native tongue other than English at home, 44% live in linguistically isolated households; this percentage drops to 9% among the 1975-1979 cohort. Retention of the native language seems strong, however, and its attrition has moved very slowly. In 1990, 96% of the recent cohort spoke a language other than English at home, and the percentage of Haitians who reported still speaking that language after 10 years in the United States remains high—85%.

Next we examine data that consider English proficiency, whether a language other than English is spoken at home, and family income simultaneously. Table 7.4 (this volume) shows a general trend for 16- to 18-year-old foreign-born youth of lower and higher family income levels that holds across 15 race, ethnic, and nationality groups. This trend is that lack of spoken English proficiency generally increases the likelihood of becoming a dropout. For all foreign-born children, among children who are poor English speakers—those who speak a language other than English and do not speak English very well—the school dropout rates are high regardless of income level (31%). Among high-income children, dropout rates are similar for both children who speak English only and those who are bilingual speakers—those who speak English very well and also speak a language other than English at home. Among low-income children, those who reported speaking English very well and also speaking a language other than English, however, have lower dropout rates (12%) than children who speak English only (15%).

These two different patterns distinguished by family income level hold for Jamaican and African immigrant children, but not for Haitian children. Lacking English proficiency is likely to be a major obstacle for Haitian youth in finishing high school; among youth reporting a spoken English problem, 13% from lower-income families and 18% from higher-income families dropped out of school. No significant distinction occurs in the dropout rates between bilingual and English-only speakers among youth from low-income Haitian families, but among youth from higher-income families, bilingual speakers drop out more than monolingual English speakers (7% vs. 0).

The percentages for Jamaicans are less reliable because the number of Jamaican immigrant children who fall into that category is very small; these data are thus uninterpretable. The data for African black immigrant children show a more typical pattern: Among youth from low-income families, 12% of English-only speakers dropped out of school, compared to 9% among bilingual speakers. No difference occurred in the dropout rates between the two groups among high-income children.

No Jamaican children fall into the category of dropouts with the least education, less than 5 years of schooling, but the percentage of Haitian children in this category who do not speak English very well is moderately high, 3% of lower-income families and 5% of higher-income families, compared to other black groups.

Conclusions

In summary, black immigrant children perform well by most educational measures and compared to the native-born population of the same age. They are not only doing well in comparison to many immigrant groups, but they are doing better in U.S. schools than native-born black children and youth. This is consistent with findings in the study by Rong, Brown, and Guo (1996) that foreign-born black children compared favorably to native-born children with two native-born parents of the same race and ethnic group in average years of schooling and school completion at all educational levels.

Although some elements of our findings can be explained partially by all three models of adaptation, these findings are not entirely consistent with any one of the three models and tend to fit more with cultural ecological and selective-assimilation models than with the classic assimilation model. The positive effects of assimilation are reflected by the English acquisition progress made by black immigrant children with longer U.S. residence and by the reduction in dropout rates with an increasing length of U.S. residence for some cohorts. This confirms what is taken to be common knowledge: Longer residence in the United States increases exposure to English and familiarity with U.S. schools and other social institutions, which in turn may lead to higher educational attainment. This model may fit other groups better, however, Hispanic immigrants rather than blacks.

Lower educational attainment among native-born African and Caribbean black youth is consistent with predictions of cultural ecology and reproduction theories. For blacks, unlike most other groups, subsequent generations of U.S. residence seem to engender more, rather than less, discrimination because immigrant blacks are not incorporated into mainstream America, but more likely to join an indigenous minority group that is highly stigmatized. Nevertheless, although a majority of newly immigrated blacks experience racial discrimination in the United States, they may perceive it differently because most of them came from countries where social class may matter more than race. Black immigrant youths tend to see themselves as immigrants and believe that accepting an American black identity may mean the acceptance of the oppositional character of that identity (Foner, 1987). They believe that an immigrant nationality identity may protect them from negative stereotypes and prevent them from incorporation into more popular but less motivated groups in school. This may explain why foreign-born black children have done better than native-born black children and some earlier immigrant cohorts.

Selective assimilation may be the key to why black immigrant youth have more schooling than black domestic youth, as well as why the effects of length of U.S. residence on attainment are different for Caribbean and African black youths. Because they have been socialized in societies with black majorities and relatively successful economic role models among their peers, black Caribbean immigrants may have a justification for a greater achievement motivation that native-born urban African Americans lack (Matthijs, 1996). The success of black immigrants may also lie in the strength of their immigrant families and communities, which instill and embody unique human, cultural, and social capital in youth. Portes and Zhou (1993) argue that the mode of incorporation of the first generation into U.S. society creates different opportunities and cultural and social capital in the form of ethnic jobs, networks, and values that create different pulls on the allegiances of children. Jamaicans' and Haitians' strong ethnic networks may generate social capital: Networks of social ties from church, neighborhood, and voluntary organizations create ties to job opportunities, as well as interwoven connections that reinforce parental authority and values. These groups resist full assimilation and consequently provide better opportunities for their children. Lacking such resources and networks, many native inner-city black children immerse themselves culturally, socially, and psychologically in the U.S. urban youth popular culture, with its strong antischool and antimainstream elements (cf. Fordham, 1996). These findings also show that improvement in English helps schooling in most cases; however, speaking a language other than English may not be an impediment to children's schooling, and bilingualism may help children do better. This may legitimize the preferences of many parents of immigrant children for offering bilingualism and biculturalism in U.S. schools.

Resistance to rapid Americanization is hard for any immigrant, but it is particularly difficult for lower-class youth who live in the inner city, influenced by television culture, youth popular culture, and peer pressure. This difficulty is compounded by pressures from whites and some blacks to make immigrant cultures invisible under the name of assimilation. Ethnographic studies indicate that black youth who choose an immigrant identity may face overwhelming pressure in school and the workplace to identify themselves only as "blacks." Additional problems arise for those U.S.-born children of immigrant parents who want to maintain their national identity. Haitian children who came to the United States at a very young age are most often seen by others as merely "black Americans," because they have developed American English proficiency and lack their parents' distinctive accents. Some of them must work actively to assert their ethnic identities (Waters, 1994).

Therefore, educators and other professionals need to be aware of immigrant black children's problems and help their identity transformations and reconstructions. Educators also need to understand the causes and rationales of these four different identities: national, pannational, pan-racial, and American. This helps inner-city immigrant minority youths to reduce the disadvantages of being both minority and immigrants in the U.S. education system. Although Caribbean immigrant parents may transmit their orientation toward hard work and achievement by emphasizing the importance of schooling for their children, intergenerational influences may be amplified and enhanced by cooperation and reinforcement from educators and other authorities who work with immigrant students in educational settings (Fernandez-Kelly & Schauffler, 1994).

Over extended periods in U.S. history, hostile reception to immigrants, including forced rapid assimilation and demands for cultural homogeneity, has had severe personal and social consequences—inner turmoil, identity crises, antagonism, behavioral problems, and social dismemberment. New immigrant black people need not be relegated to the urban underclass if we give enough attention to the lessons of the past. Educators and other agents of U.S. society have choices that may ease the transition or hamper it.

10

The Future for Immigrant Students

Migration is likely to increase rather than to decrease in the 1990s because of uneven population and economic growth, global economic restructuring, and other factors. Today, only a limited basis exists for international cooperation on migration. What should the industrial democracies do about rising migration pressures? No one knows whether the immigrants arriving in industrial democracies today will become well-integrated fellow citizens or join an oppressed underclass. But immigration is changing the industrial democracies.

Throughout much of human history, complex societies have had a pyramid shape: a tiny elite on the top and poor masses at the bottom. The immigrants arriving in the industrial democracies today, when assessed by the best single predictor of economic success, years of education, have an hourglass or barbell shape: They are more likely than the native born to have more than a college degree, and they are more likely to have less than a high school diploma. One of the challenges facing countries receiving immigrants is how to ensure that the children of immigrants of all educational levels have the same opportunities as the children of native-born parents.

Difficult problems can lead to bad policies. But doing nothing about rising immigration and ignoring integration problems are likely to be worse. If the status quo continues, large numbers of unskilled immigrants will arrive in industrial countries, generating support for politicians and policies that assign a low priority to the integration of immigrants and their children. The industrial democracies must meet the twin challenges of migration—managing the entry of newcomers and integrating the foreigners in their midst.

For most Americans, education is the key to a good job and a promising future. Enhancing the education of those currently marginalized is crucial for their socioeconomic advancement as well as for the active participation of the United States in the global economy of the 21st century. The stages of assimilation common to previous waves of immigrants may no longer occur: The first generation began at the bottom of the ladder and struggled, the second generation climbed, and the third generation attended a university and entered the U.S. mainstream. Today, the increasing number and variety of people of diverse ethnicities and cultures are transforming the mainstream: Those once marginalized are causing the majority to adapt. Some newcomers start right at the top of the ladder. Immigration policy must recognize the range of resources that people bring with them (Portes & Rumbaut, 1996).

Recommendations

Our findings are consistent with recent social science research: The patterns emerging from this study have been documented elsewhere by the scholarly community although they may not be widely recognized by the public. We summarize recommendations derived from the findings into the following three categories.

First, the common notion that more "Americanization" is always better for educational attainment discourages consideration of alternative approaches to assimilation being used successfully by today's immigrants. Selective assimilation and bilingualism are examples of these.

Second, immigrants have actually revived some urban areas. They put new demands on urban schools but also transfuse new blood into the system. An influx of immigrant minorities, especially children of immigrants, can sometimes lift attainment for urban schools. Although the entry of pupils from immigrant communities poses new challenges for educational institutions, the transition can also contribute to enrollment and attainment growth and other constructive changes. Immigrant blacks and their communities stimulate the substandardized urban schools with their strong motivation for education, their different ideas on parenting and schooling, and different attitudes and psychology toward racial discrimination and how to challenge social and financial disadvantages.

Third, this study on the similarities and differences in educational attainment among various immigrant groups provides further evidence of the significant effects of the complex and dynamic interactions among students' multiple statuses of social class, race, ethnicity, nationality, and length of residence on their language adaptation and schooling. Newcomers from more advantaged educational and occupational backgrounds do better on the average, but often individual resources interact with the social context that receives them (Portes & Schauffler, 1994). Immigrants from rural and nonliterate communities may take more generations to succeed in education than do others, but their grandchildren do well if not hampered by such barriers as structural inequities. Likewise, immigrants whose cultures of origin prize literacy and family stability—many Asians and Jews, for example—may be predisposed to do well in U.S. schools, but individuals in these groups have also been limited by discrimination.

Educators, social workers, and other professionals who work with immigrant children need to understand that assimilation is a process through which immigrant groups gradually become integrated into the adopted society. The process is complex, however, laden with conflict and stress. For many immigrant children, especially racial minority children such as blacks, the outcomes are uncertain. If these children lose their cultural heritage through assimilation, many may become vulnerable to identifying with the antischool culture of inner-city communities, in which case not only may they suffer oppression as individuals, but their local communities and our national society will lose a potential for transformation.

Classroom and School Issues

We have discussed the educational performance of immigrant children and how personal and contextual factors affect the educational outcomes of these newcomers. We now address some specific issues relevant to immigrant children's education in U.S. schools.

School policy toward immigrant students and teachers' classroom practices affect immigrant students' adjustment and adaptation to U.S. school systems (e.g., Blakely, 1983; Dentler & Hafner, 1997). When immigrant students move to regular classes after the first one or two "special" semesters, they usually receive no further extra help, which may explain their high rates of failure and dropping out of school. In many schools in the South and other regions where immigrants have been rare, no help is offered to these newcomers. These students depend profoundly on their academic preparation prior to immigration (cf. Macias, 1990). Many children, however, come to school unprepared. Without considerable professional help, immigrant children who enter elementary school at Grade 4 or above have serious problems catching up with regular instruction. Whether they overcome initial difficulties depends on their parents' education, family socioeconomic status, race and ethnicity, and country of origin. Students who attended school full-time in their native countries are often ahead of U.S. students, especially in math and science (McDonnell & Hill, 1993). Students whose schooling was delayed or disrupted because of poverty and war, however, are often far behind. Students from rural areas of Asia, Africa, and Central America may arrive at elementary school not knowing how to use a pencil or eraser, virtually illiterate, and unable to perform basic computation in their native languages. Without a comprehensive educational policy, flexible school planning, and a team of faculty and staff members knowledgeable about, willing to handle, and capable of managing the complicated situation and diverse needs of today's immigrant students, more failures and more dropouts are probable. Younger and younger people may join the illiterate and semiliterate population, to be trapped there for life. This betrays the American dream.

Attending high school for a recently immigrated youth is a different experience than attending elementary school. The difficulties for immigrant youth at this level transcend language challenges. High school social life is brutal in the eyes of many native-born youth and even some sophisticated adults. Adolescent newcomers struggle in high school, but may be marginalized and rejected in a strange environment with no friends, no helpful adults, and no relevant past schooling experience to shape and reshape their behavior. Few teachers are immigrants themselves, especially in areas of the United States with recent immigration history. Immigrant parents often are unaware of and unable to understand their children's problems; most of them have never had any educational experience in U.S. elementary and secondary schools, and the educational systems they experienced in their native countries were more traditional and very different from that in this country.

One solution to these issues is a newcomers' school (McDonnell & Hill, 1993) where recently immigrated children can get organized and become fully prepared and well trained for U.S. schools, a place to help them make a fresh start and to ease the initial transition. Teachers in newcomer high schools can pay greater attention to curriculum development than do those in traditional schools, readapting curricula to a constantly changing student body that differs from year to year in students' countries of origin and academic skill levels. The philosophy of newcomer schools, with a dual emphasis on cultural acclimation and academic achievement tailored to a wide variety of skill levels, means that the curriculum is more integrated across academic subjects than is typical in most high schools. This is the opposite of the "sink or swim" policy directing U.S. educational policy toward immigrants for more than a century.

Teachers who have had experience working with immigrant children change their lesson design, teaching strategies, note taking, testing, and homework assignments. Compared with native readers, a higher percentage of immigrant children are slow English readers and visual learners. This may be particularly true among Asian students. A higher percentage of Asian students are recent immigrants who may have problems reading in English. Data collected by the National Center for Educational Statistics (U.S. Department of Education, 1993a) show that Asian students do well in math and have more interest and skills in computer technologies. Using visuals and interactive instructional technology to teach Asian American students may be more efficient than more traditional instructional approaches.

Academic accomplishment is only one positive outcome of schooling. Despite the academic success of some, many Asian students continue to experience feelings of inferiority, alienation, and social isolation in school (Bowler, Rausch, & Schwarzer, 1986; Gibson, 1988; Greene, 1987). Psychologists and sociologists have reported severe problems in development of ethnic identity and ethnic attitude among Asian youth (Huang & Ying, 1989; Katz, 1987; Moscovici & Paicheler, 1978; Sue & Sue, 1973). School psychologists, consultants, and other social service staff members may have no background or experience working with Asian children and families. More in-service training and recruitment of Asian aides are needed (Bowler et al., 1986; Gordon & Friedenberg, 1988).

Language Issues

Language difficulties for immigrant students remain enormous, especially for middle or high school students who attend regular classes but speak no English. Many young people may know some English but not speak it in classrooms for fear of being ridiculed by peers and criticized by teachers. Both of us have had many years of experience supervising student teachers; we have had the opportunity to observe hundreds of classrooms at various grade levels in several states. We do not recall even once hearing a student with an foreign accent ask or answer questions in these classrooms or make any short or long oral presentations. Because of this silence, recent immigrants become invisible. How do these young people keep everything to themselves for 6 hours a day and 185 days a year? Do they want to say something, or do they just completely withdraw?

As educators committed to public schooling, we believe it is crucial to children's self-image and self-confidence to be able to ask and answer questions and present solutions to problems in front of their teachers and peers. For this reason alone we believe that adjustments made by classroom teachers to instructional strategies, evaluation sys tems, and classroom management to involve immigrant students actively are indispensable. Furthermore, some immigrant students' apparent fluency in oral English often conceals their slow progress in mastery of the written language, and that may cause major problems for immigrant students and for school personnel. We have observed, as classroom teachers and college professors, that most recent immigrant students in middle and high school are insufficiently fluent in English to take instruction in math, science, social studies, and reading. They have to make extraordinary efforts to keep up with their classmates. Aside from a one-hour ESL class, they rarely receive any other aids from teachers in subject fields. For many immigrant youths, low educational attainment may be a product of their low levels of English language proficiency as well as an outcome of their unsatisfactory social life in schools.

We have no doubt of the value of acquiring English proficiency for newly immigrated people from non-English-speaking nations. Among early 20th-century immigrants, the shift to English as an individual's chief language typically occurred over three generations. Immigrants rarely developed full English proficiency during their lifetimes. The children of these immigrants were often bilingual, using their parents' language at home and English at school, with English often dominant as they joined the mainstream workforce. Their children—the third generation to be born in the United States with two American-born parents—were usually monolingual English speakers. As U.S. society moves to a high technology and high service information society, however, the three-generation shift to English may be compressed to two generations (Martin & Midgley, 1994). Our findings on language evolution within the first generation of immigrant children supports bilingualism. Although the majority of immigrant children still speak the language of their native tongues at home after 10 or 15 years of U.S. residency, less than a fifth of these children remained in linguistically isolated households and more than three quarters of these children developed oral English proficiency within that time period.

Although immigrants and their children may acquire English faster than in the past, they may not learn it fast enough for contemporary conditions. The difficulties for immigrants who have not yet developed English proficiency have increased. At the beginning of the 20th century, immigrants were employed in many blue-collar jobs that did not require English; in today's service-dominated economy, it is almost impossible to support a family adequately without mastery of English. One recent study reported that immigrant men speaking a language other than English at home and not fluent in English earned half as much as their English-fluent counterparts (Meisenheimer, 1992).

U.S. educators may continue to debate whether public schools are obligated to help immigrant children retain their native languages. But, few question the necessity for schools to help these children improve their English proficiency in ESL class or in various forms of bilingual classes. ESL and other services for helping immigrant children improve their English, however, are usually inadequate, inappropriate, and inconsistent.

McDonnell and Hill (1993) cite a California state department of education taskforce, reporting that in 1989 the state had a shortage of 11,710 bilingual teachers. The absolute numbers were greatest for Spanish; only half of the more than 600,000 Spanish-speaking children in Cali-

fornia were taught by a teacher who spoke Spanish, with the state esti-
mating that the shortage of Spanish bilingual teachers was close to
8,000. But the need was also high in other languages, such as Vietnamese, for which 716 teachers were needed, with only 46 then available.
Similarly, the state education department in New York reported in 1990
that 32% of the ESL teachers in the state and 48% of the bilingual teachers lacked the appropriate certification. Approximately 2.4 million children, including native-born children with foreign-born parents, of limited English proficiency (LEP) were identified in the United States in
1982 (U.S. Department of Education, 1984). In addition to federal funds
for bilingual education, which in 1983 served 234,000 students, more
than a dozen states required programs for LEP children; nevertheless,
an estimated 1.5 to 1.8 million children remained to be served.

Most school districts are able to hire some bilingual aides —immigrants or U.S.-born adults who speak the children's home language but
who do not have teaching credentials (Abascal-Hildebrand, 1994;
McDonnell & Hill, 1993). Some of these aides are well-educated and can
substitute effectively for teachers, whereas others have little education
and can provide only custodial care and rough translation. Nevertheless, they all help children's language transition process by improving
classroom communication, promoting students' English learning skills,
and implicitly encouraging children to maintain their native languages.

Related to the shortage of qualified ESL school personnel is the
problem of assessing immigrant students' English for initial placement
and later progress. Immigrant student intake centers are far from per-
fect; teachers across the country complain that assessments of students'
language and skill development are often flawed. Centers dealing with
multiple language groups are particularly prone to errors. But, alternative informal assessments done by overworked schoolteachers are apparently much worse. Assessment centers are essential if a district in-
tends to assign immigrant students individually to the schools best
equipped to meet their needs (McDonnell & Hill, 1993). In addition to
a thorough evaluation of immigrant students' English language proficiency, assessments are also necessary of student performance in other
subject areas and of educational background and career goals.

A common misconception is that new immigrants do not want
their children to learn English. Most immigrants realize that the ability
to speak English is the key to their children's advancement and in-
volvement in U.S. society. Although we do not deny variations between
and within country-origin groups in immigrants' knowledge of English,

in their perception of English adaptation, and subsequently in their willingness and ability to learn English (Fawcett, Carino, Park, & Garden, 1990), we also note a survey of U.S. residents of Mexican, Cuban, and Puerto Rican origins recording more than 90% agreement that "all U.S. citizens and residents should learn English" (Martin & Midgley, 1994).

The issue over which some immigrant parents battle with schools is not an opposition to their children learning English, but their desire for children to retain their first language in addition to learning English. Maintaining both languages and both cultures has been a privilege reserved for higher-class white European immigrants. Adult immigrants from Germany and France may obtain professional and management jobs without significantly giving up their languages and other cultural traditions and without resentment from the U.S. native white population. They may also deliberately choose to maintain their children's bilingual and bicultural status when they observe how hard white upper-middle-class families are trying to furnish their children with a language other than English and the experience of exposure to foreign cultures.

Success or failure in English acquisition depends on more than an isolated individual's efforts. Effort is one aspect of acculturation in the social and cultural context in which learning English happens; to a large extent the context determines the outcome of this learning. Many educators believe that individual variation in necessity, ability, and motivation cause major differences in language adaptation. This assumption, however, is increasingly challenged by sociologists. An immigrant's opportunity to assimilate, either culturally or structurally, is limited by the joint effect of ethnicity and social class. Immigrants from Third World rural areas, with little education and few material possessions in their native countries, are likelier to stay at the bottom of social or occupational strata in their new country; they more commonly live in a racially or linguistically segregated neighborhood and are employed in an ethnically saturated job—a situation wherein disproportionate numbers of a given minority work in a given occupation—that offers little socioeconomic advancement. Their children may receive inferior education from schools not comparable to schools located in more affluent white neighborhoods. As a consequence of this initial disadvantage, these immigrants and their children may have less opportunity to learn English and to observe and integrate with middle-class U.S. culture. Sociolinguists maintain that the education of language minority students, including the learning of effective English, can be understood only within the larger sociocultural context of schools and the society within which they function (Heath, 1986). Knowing how these instrumental factors operate prevents us from attributing English proficiency problems among immigrants to merely these newcomers' stubbornness, arrogance, or unwillingness to learn English. Although we are on the peak of the fourth wave of immigration to the United States, government at all levels has not provided adequate services to help newcomers learn English. About a million people are enrolled in public adult-education English classes. Community-based organizations and volunteer literacy organizations around the country also teach English to foreigners. All of these organizations report a large unmet need for more classes, especially at times and in places convenient for working people. No federally financed program exists to teach English, although states have the option of using federal adult-education money for that purpose (McDonnell & Hill, 1993).

In the 200-year history of the United States, language differences have often been a major source of tension between newcomers and established residents. Bach (1993) emphasizes the intergroup conflict, tensions, and distance resulting when people are unable to communicate with each other. At the same time, language can serve as a primary method of bringing people together. The key is how we understand the issue and whether we handle it properly.

The Future of Immigration and U.S. Schools

Challenges from continued immigration face the United States in many areas, affecting the future of this country and its relations with other countries. According to the U.S. Bureau of the Census (1996), if immigration continues at present levels, a population exceeding 300 million in 20 years and reaching 370 million by 2040 can be projected (see Figure 10.1). By 2040, the proportion of the minority population may rise to 40%, and one of three residents may be either an immigrant or a child of immigrants. This large-scale immigration will affect all aspects of life over the next 50 years, and U.S. schools will continue to be the front line for meeting newcomers. Because immigration accounts for one third of the U.S. population growth, schools in areas of increasing population may expect an overflow of immigrant children, especially the Sunbelt states whose service organizations and personnel have historically had

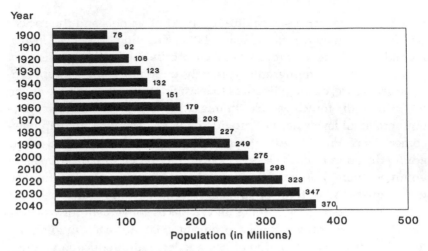

Year

Figure 10.1. U.S. Population, 1900-2040

SOURCE: U.S. Bureau of the Census (1996).

very little emotional or material preparation for working with immigrants. Two important demographic aspects of future population change—generational and racial-ethnic—must be considered.

First, immigrants will become even more prevalent over the next 50 years. A huge wave of immigrants entered the United States in the late 1980s and early 1990s. This peaked in 1991, when a record 1.8 million people were legally admitted. The number of immigrants, currently at an all-time high of 23.2 million, will increase to about 50 million in 2040. The percentage of foreign born in the population will increase steadily from 8.5% and will begin to level off at about 14% by about 2030, or about 1 in 7 Americans, the same proportion of immigrants as occurred in the late-19th and early-20th century. The second generation, also now near an all-time high of 25 million, will grow to about 45 million by 2040. At that time, immigrants and the children of immigrants will account for slightly more than one quarter of the U.S population.

High levels of immigration are expected to amplify the relatively high rate of minority population growth. Current projections anticipate a net addition of 880,000 immigrants a year until 2050, composed of about 324,000 Hispanics, 323,000 non-Hispanic Asians, 174,000 non-Hispanic whites, and 60,000 non-Hispanic blacks. The compounding effect on annual immigration at these levels is causing the projected rise in the proportion of minorities in the population from 25% in 1990 to

47% in 2050. According to these projections, by 2050, non-Hispanic whites will account for one half the population, while Asians and Hispanics will form nearly one third.

According to Passel and Edmonston (1992), the composition of the minority population will also change steadily. In 1990, about one quarter of the population was minority, with 12% of the total population being black, 9% being Hispanic, 3% being Asian, and less than 1% being Native American. The black proportion of the U.S. population is expected to rise from its current 12% to 13.5% in 2040 and will constitute less than one third of the minority population. The percentage of blacks will remain in the 12%-14% range throughout the 21st century. Hispanics will become the largest minority group in 2020, however, at about 15% of the population. In 2040, the Hispanic population may reach 64.3 million, almost triple its current size (22.4 million), and may comprise 18% of the total U.S. population. If current trends continue, in less than 50 years, one of every five Americans will be of Hispanic origin. The Asian population also will continue to grow, largely because of immigration. The Asian American population may reach 23 million (the size of 1990's Hispanic population) and triple its current level (7.3 million) in less than 30 years. It will rise to 35 million in 2040; one of every 10 Americans will be Asian.

Current demographic data indicate that the United States is once again on the eve of large ethnic transformations. In the past, major ethnic changes in the pattern of immigration have given rise to social disturbances, followed by periods of adaptation and integration of the immigrants and adjustments by U.S. society. The new phase has already provoked disturbances and raised questions about "American" identity (e.g., Hunter, 1991).

These population trends have tremendous implications for and applications to U.S. educational planners and policymakers, as well as principals and teachers at all levels of local school systems. Because the new immigrant wave is multidimensional and multifaceted in demographic, social, political, and cultural characteristics, schools need to develop more ways to achieve integration during the next century, a period of heavy immigration. Whether the United States succeeds with the new immigrants as well as it has done before depends on how we, Americans as a whole, continue to answer honestly and fairly these fundamental questions: Who have we been, who are we now, who do we want to be, and who will we be? As U.S. educators, we have to answer those questions with hand, heart, and mind.

As Ravitch (1974) observes, the descendants of the miserably poor Eastern Europeans who overflowed the urban schools in the 19th and early-20th centuries are today the prosperous middle class of the city and its suburbs. The American myth of the self-made individual, going from rags to riches through hard work and virtue, has often been achieved in the United States, and it remains the dream of today's immigrants and their children. The poignant memories of many old Chinese immigrants have been assuaged by what they see now: Chinese Americans, as an ethnic group, now constitute one of the highest percentage of university graduates and professionals in the country (U.S. Bureau of the Census, 1983b). Despite the language barriers and the hardship of a new life in a strange land, in the minds of many newly immigrated Hispanic, Asian, and black youths, America is still a golden gate, and social mobility through hard work and education remains possible (Lindsey, 1985). Every day, more than 1,000 children from foreign countries enter our schools and walk into our classrooms. They look at us with fresh and anxious young faces full of hope: Are you going to help us fulfill our dream?

Sources of
Information

The content of this book is based on statistical information and on the work of many researchers and theorists from a variety of disciplines. The statistical information is census data that describes the present status of immigrant children aged 5-18 years in the United States. The terms *children* and *youth* are used throughout this book to include individuals from childhood to adolescence.

In this section, we describe the 1990 census data and the data analysis methods we have used. Census data, data collected by the National Center for Educational Statistics, and data from other sources are used for analyses. The most comprehensive and up-to-date information comes from the 1990 census, including aggregated data and individual data.

Sources of Data

The major data source we have used is the PUMS 5% (Public Use Microdata Samples), which contains records representing 5% of the housing units in the United States and the persons in them. It is the largest population sample ever used in educational research, giving us records for approximately 12.5 million persons and more than 5 million housing units.

The PUMS is a stratified subsample of the full census sample, approximately 15.9% of all housing units that received census long-form questionnaires. Census analysts have used a stratified systematic selection procedure with equal probability to select subjects for the microdata samples. They have sampled housing unit by housing unit to allow study of family relationships and housing unit characteristics.

The PUMS 5% file consists of two types of records: housing and persons. Each housing unit record is followed by a variable number of person records, one for each member of the housing unit or none if vacant. Because the sample provides data for all persons living in a sampled household, we can study how characteristics of household members are interrelated: for example, income, educational attainment, and linguistic status of parents, other adults, and children. The PUMS 5% contains individual weights for each person and housing unit, which, when applied to the individual records, expand the sample to the total population.

Variables

The variables attached to the records are characteristics of individuals, of households or microsystems, and of environments or macrosystems. We list these characteristics next.

Individual level: Physical characteristics include age, gender, race/ethnicity, marital status, and number of children. Sociocultural characteristics included educational enrollment, years of school completed, ability to speak English, ability to speak a language other than English at home, year of immigration, citizenship status, and employment.

Microsystem level: Cultural characteristics include household language, linguistic isolation status, English proficiency of parents, and length of residence in the United States of parents. Socioeconomic characteristics include such information as parental education and occupation, type of family, size of family, family income, and poverty status.

Macrosystem level: Geographic location is represented by region, division, state, county, and tract. Communities are characterized by size and location as rural, urban, central city, and suburban.

In our study, a person who did not have a high school diploma and was not enrolled in school in 1990 has been defined as a school dropout. The 1990 census is the first decennial census with questions allowing persons to report the completion of the 12th grade without receiving a high school diploma or the equivalent (GED).

Data Analysis

Researchers have reported great variation within such supernationality groups as Hispanic, Asian, and black immigrants. We have worked with such a large manipulatable census database that we can examine with fairly adequate numbers educational attainment and such issues as dropout behavior among the immigrant youth in each subgroup.

In analyzing individual, microsystem, and macrosystem factors to address the school dropout problem, for example, we have used simple descriptive statistics. Means and percentage tables often suffice in a report of this kind. For more information about sample design and sampling and nonsampling errors, see the technical documents provided by the U.S. Bureau of the Census we have listed as references.

The following clarifications may help in evaluating our data analysis and interpreting the results:

1. In the PUMS 5% sample, schooling attainment is reported as actual years of school completed only for ninth grade and above. Prior to that, attainment is reported in broader categories by level of schooling completed (for example, no school, completion of 5 years' schooling, or completion of 8 years' schooling).
2. To measure the years of school completed and schooling completion at various levels, we use the narrowly defined term *educational attainment* to distinguish from broader terms such as *achievement* or *accomplishment*, which may include grade point averages and other educational assessment indicators. A group with higher educational attainment in our report does not necessarily possess higher grades, test scores, or other indicators of educational success.
3. Psychological, philosophical, and motivational questions (e.g., youth motivation, youth and parental aspirations, perception of labor market opportunities, attraction to "oppositional" cultures, and the like) are traditionally excluded from census questionnaires.

References

Abascal-Hildebrand, M. L. D. (1994, April). *Asian paraprofessional in-service: Ethnography as a means for promoting participation and recruiting teachers.* Paper presented at the annual meeting of the American Educational Research Association, New Orleans, LA.

Alatis, J., & Staczek, J. (1985). *Perspectives on bilingualism and bilingual education.* Washington, DC: Georgetown University Press.

Anisef, P. (1975). Consequences of ethnicity for educational plans among grade 12 students. In A. Wolfgang (Ed.), *Education of immigrant students* (pp. 122-136). Toronto: Ontario Institute for Studies in Education.

Anzovin, S. (Ed.). (1985). *The problem of immigration.* New York: H. W. Wilson.

Arias, M. B. (1986). The context of education for Hispanic students: An overview. *American Journal of Education, 95*(1), 26-57.

Bach, R. (1993). *Changing relations.* New York: Ford Foundation.

Barringer, H. R., Gardner, R. W., & Levin, M. J. (1993). *Asians and Pacific Islanders.* New York: Russell Sage.

Bartel, A. P. (1989). Where do the new U.S. immigrants live? *Journal of Labor Economics, 7*(4), 317-391.

Blakely, M. M. (1983). Southeast Asian refugee parents: An inquiry into home-school communication and understanding. *Anthropology and Education Quarterly, 14*(1), 43-68.

Bloom, D. E., & Brender, A. (1993). Labor and the emerging world economy. *Population Bulletin, 48*(2), 2-40.

Bohannan, P. (1995). *How culture works.* New York: Free Press.

Bowler, R., Rausch, S., & Schwarzer, R. (1986). Self-esteem and interracial attitudes in black high school students: A comparison with five other ethnic groups. *Urban Education, 21*(1), 3-17.

Butcher, K. (1994). Black immigrants to the United States: A comparison with native blacks and other immigrants. *Industrial and Labor Relations Review, 47,* 265-284.

Caplan, N., Choy, M. H., & Whitmore, J. K. (1991). *Children of the boat people: A study of educational success.* Ann Arbor: University of Michigan Press.

Carrasquillo, A. L. (1991). *Hispanic children and youth in the United States.* New York: Garland.

Carrithers, M. (1992). *Why humans have cultures: Explaining anthropology and social diversity.* Oxford, UK: Oxford University Press.

Chaze, W. (1985). Invasion from Mexico: It just keeps growing. In S. Anzovin (Ed.), *The problem of immigration* (pp. 39-45). New York: H. W. Wilson.

Chinchilla, N., Hamilton, N., & Loucky, J. (1993). Central Americans in Los Angeles: An immigrant community in transition. In J. Moore & R. Pinderhughes (Eds.), *In the barrios: Latinos and the underclass debate* (pp. 51-78). New York: Russell Sage.

Collins, J. (1988). Language and class in minority education. *Anthropology and Education Quarterly, 19,* 299-326.

Conley, S., & Baumann, M. (1993, July 14). Immigration: Tracking the quest for freedom. *USA Today,* p. 1.

Cornbleth, C., & Waugh, D. (1995). *The great speckled bird: Multicultural politics and education policy making.* New York: St. Martin's.

Cubberley, E. P. (1909). *Changing conceptions of education.* New York: Houghton-Mifflin.

Davis, M. P. (1990). *Mexican voices/American dreams: An oral history of Mexican immigration to the United States.* New York: Henry Holt.

Delgado-Gaitan, C. (1988). The value of conformity: Learning to stay in school. *Anthropology and Education Quarterly, 19,* 354-381.

Delgado-Gaitan, C., & Trueba, H. (1991). *Crossing cultural borders: Education for immigrant families in America.* London: Falmer.

Del Pinal, J. (1993). *We the American Hispanics.* Washington, DC: U.S. Bureau of the Census.

Dentler, R. A., & Hafner, A. L. (1997). *Hosting newcomers.* New York: Teachers College Press.

Duran, R. (1983). *Hispanic education and background.* New York: College Entrance Examination Board.

Edmonston, B., & Passel, J. S. (1992). *Immigration and immigrant generations in population projections.* Washington, DC: Urban Institute.

Erickson, F. (1987). Transformation and school success: The politics and culture of educational achievement. *Anthropology and Education Quarterly, 18,* 335-365.

Espiritu, Y. L. (1992). *Asian American panethnicity: Bridging institutions and identities.* Philadelphia: Temple University Press.

Farley, R., & Walter, R. A. (1989). *The color line and the quality of life in America.* Oxford, UK: Oxford University Press.

Farrell, J. J. (1980). *The immigrant and the school in New York City.* New York: Arno.

Fawcett, J. T., Carino, B. V., Park, I. H., & Garden, R. W. (1990). *Selectivity and diversity: The effects of U.S. immigration policy on immigrant characteristics.* Paper presented at the annual meeting of the Population Association of America, Toronto, Canada.

Fernandez-Kelly, M. P., & Schauffler, R. (1994). Divided fates: Immigrant children in a restructured U.S. economy. *International Migration Review, 28*(4), 662-689.

Ferris, E. G. (1987). *The Central American refugees.* New York: Praeger.

Foley, D. E. (1991). Reconsidering anthropological explanations of ethnic school failure. *Anthropology and Education Quarterly, 22*(1), 60-86.

Foner, N. (1987). The Jamaicans: Race and ethnicity among migrants in New York City. In N. Foner (Ed.), *New immigrants in New York City* (pp. 131-158). New York: Columbia University Press.

Fordham, S. (1996). *Blacked out: Dilemmas of race, identity, and success at Capital High.* Chicago: University of Chicago Press.

Fosnot, C. T. (Ed.). (1996). *Constructivism: Theory, perspectives, and practice.* New York: Teachers College Press.

Fraser, S. (Ed.). (1995). *The bell curve wars: Race, intelligence, and the future of America.* New York: Basic Books.

Gardner, R. W., Robey, B., & Smith, P. C. (1985). Asian Americans: Growth, change, and diversity. *Population Bulletin, 40*(4), 3-43.

Gibson, M. A. (1988). *Accommodation without assimilation: Sikh immigrants in an American high school.* Ithaca, NY: Cornell University Press.

Gibson, M. A., & Bhachu, P. K. (1991). The dynamics of educational decision making: A comparative case study of Sikhs in Britain and the United States. In M. A. Gibson & J. U. Ogbu (Eds.), *Minority status and schooling: A comparative study of immigrant and involuntary minorities* (pp. 63-95). New York: Garland.

Gibson, M. A., & Ogbu, J. U. (Eds.). (1991). *Minority status and schooling: A comparative study of immigrant and involuntary minorities.* New York: Garland.

Glazer, N. (1977). Jewish Americans. In M. J. Gold, C. A. Grant, & H. N. Rivlin (Eds.), *In praise of diversity: A resource book for multicultural education* (pp. 163-175). Washington, DC: Teacher Corps, Association of Teacher Educators.

Goetz, J. P., & Grant, L. (1988). Conceptual approaches to studying gender in schools. *Anthropology and Education Quarterly, 19*, 182-196.

Goode, J., & Schneider, J. A. (1994). *Reshaping ethnic and racial relations in Philadelphia: Immigrants in a divided city.* Philadelphia: Temple University Press.

Gordon, R. A., & Friedenberg, J. E. (1988). Asian Americans: Developing marketable skills. *Vocational Education, 63*(1), 25-27.

Goto, S. T. (1997). Nerds, normal people, and homeboys: Accommodation and resistance among Chinese American students. *Anthropology and Education Quarterly, 28*(1), 70-84.

Grant, L., & Rong, X. L. (1996). *Gender, immigrant generation, and schooling attainment by early adulthood among five ethnic groups.* Unpublished manuscript.

Greene, E. (1987, November 18). Asian-Americans find U.S. colleges insensitive, form campus organizations to fight bias. *Chronicle of Higher Education*, pp. A1, A38-A40.

Gregory, S., & Sanjek, R. (Eds.). (1994). *Race.* New Brunswick, NJ: Rutgers University Press.

Handlin, O. (1951). *The uprooted.* New York: Grosset & Dunlap.

Hansen, K. A., & Bachu, A. (1995). *The foreign-born population: 1994. Current population reports.* Washington, DC: U.S. Bureau of the Census.

Harwood, E. (1986, September). American public opinion and U.S. immigration policy. *Annals of the American Academy of Political and Social Science, 487*, 201-212.

Hatcher, R., & Troyna, B. (1993). Racialization and children. In C. McCarthy & W. Crichlow (Eds.), *Race, identity, and representation in education* (pp. 109-125). New York: Routledge.

Hayes, K. G. (1992). Attitudes toward education: Voluntary and involuntary immigrants from the same families. *Anthropology and Education Quarterly, 23*, 250-267.

Heath, S. B. (1983). *Ways with words: Language, life, and work in communities and classrooms.* Cambridge, UK: Cambridge University Press.

Heath, S. B. (1986). Sociocultural contexts of language development. In *Beyond language: Social and cultural factors in schooling language minority students* (pp. 143-186). Sacramento, CA: State Department of Education, Bilingual Education Office.

Hendricks, G. (1974). *The Dominican diaspora: From the Dominican Republic to New York City—Villagers in transition.* New York: Teachers College Press.

Heritage Foundation. (1985). *How immigrants affect Americans' living standard: A debate between Julian Simon and Roger Conner*. Washington, DC: Author.

Herrnstein, R. J., & Murray, C. (1994). *The bell curve: Intelligence and class structure in American life*. New York: Free Press.

Hirschman, C. (1994). Problems and prospects of studying immigrant adaptation from the 1990 population census: From federational comparisons to the process of "becoming Americans." *International Migration Review, 28*(4), 690-713.

Hirschman, C., & Falcon, L. (1985). The educational attainment of religion-ethnic groups in the United States. *Research in the Sociology of Education and Socialization, 5*, 83-120.

Hirschman, C., & Wong, M. (1986). The extraordinary educational attainment of Asian Americans: A search for historical evidence and explanations. *Social Forces, 65*(1), 1-27.

HMP (Hemispheric Migration Project), & CSUCA (Consejo Superior Universitario Centroamericano, Secretaria General). (1989). *Central American refugees*. Washington, DC: Georgetown University, Center for Immigration Policy and Refugee Assistance.

Horowitz, R. (1983). *Honor and the American dream: Culture and identity in a Chicano community*. New Brunswick, NJ: Rutgers University Press.

Hostetler, J. A., & Huntington, G. E. (1971). *Children in Amish society: Socialization and community education*. New York: Holt, Rinehart & Winston.

Howe, I. (1980). *World of our fathers*. New York: Bantam.

Hsia, J. (1988). *Asian Americans in higher education and at work*. Hillsdale, NJ: Lawrence Erlbaum.

Huang, L. N., & Ying, Y. (1989). Chinese American children and adolescents. In J. T. Gibbs & L. N. Huang (Eds.), *Children of color: Psychological interventions with minority youth* (pp. 30-66). San Francisco: Jossey-Bass.

Hudak, G. M. (1993). Technologies of marginality: Strategies of stardom and displacement in adolescent life. In C. McCarthy & W. Crichlow (Eds.), *Race, identity, and representation in education* (pp. 172-187). New York: Routledge.

Hunter, J. D. (1991). *Culture wars: The struggle to define America*. New York: Basic Books.

Igoa, C. (1995). *The inner world of the immigrant child*. New York: St. Martin's.

Jacob, E., & Jordan, C. (Eds.). (1993). *Minority education: Anthropological perspectives*. Norwood, NJ: Ablex.

Jasso, G., & Rosenzweig, M. R. (1990). *The new chosen people: Immigrants to the United States*. New York: Russell Sage.

Jiobu, R. M. (1988). *Ethnicity and assimilation*. Albany: State University of New York Press.

Johnson, H. (1968). An "internationalist" model. In W. Adams (Ed.), *The brain drain* (pp. 69-91). New York: Macmillan.

Kasinitz, P. (1992). *Caribbean New York: Black immigrants and the politics of race*. Ithaca, NY: Cornell University Press.

Katz, P. (1987). Developmental and social processes in ethnic attitudes and self-identification. In J. S. Phinney & M. J. Rotheram (Eds.), *Children's ethnic socialization* (pp. 92-100). Newbury Park, CA: Sage.

Kim, E.-Y. (1993). Career choice among second-generation Korean-Americans: Reflections of a cultural model of success. *Anthropology and Education Quarterly, 24*, 224-248.

Knight, H. (1997, April 9). U.S. immigrant level at highest point since '30s. *Los Angeles Times*, pp. A1, A14.

Konner, M. (1982). *The tangled wing: Biological constraints on the human spirit*. New York: Harper & Row.

Kuo, C.-L. (1982). Perceptions of assimilation among Chinese in the United States. In C. B. Marrett & C. Leggon (Eds.), *Research in race and ethnic relations* (pp. 127-143). London: JAI.

Lamphere, L. (Ed.). (1992). *Structuring diversity: Ethnographic perspectives on the new immigration*. Chicago: University of Chicago Press.

Lamphere, L., Stepick, A., & Grenier, G. (Eds.). (1994). *Newcomers in the workplace: Immigrants and the restructuring of the U.S. economy*. Philadelphia: Temple University Press.

Lapham, S. L. (1993). *We the American foreign born*. Washington, DC: U.S. Bureau of the Census.

La Sorte, M. (1985). *La Merica: Images of Italian greenhorn experience*. Philadelphia: Temple University Press.

Leakey, R., & Lewin, R. (1992). *Origins reconsidered: In search of what makes us human*. New York: Doubleday.

Lee, E. (1966). A theory of migration. *Demography, 3*(1), 47-57.

Lee, E. (1970). Migration in relation to education, intellect, and social structure. *Population Index, 36*(4), 437-444.

Lee, E., & Rong, X. L. (1988). The educational and economic achievement of Asian-Americans. *Elementary School Journal, 88*, 545-560.

Lee, S. J. (1994). Behind the model-minority stereotype: voices of high- and low-achieving Asian American students. *Anthropology and Education Quarterly, 25*, 413-429.

Leonard, K. I. (1992). *Making ethnic choices: California's Punjabi Mexican Americans*. Philadelphia: Temple University Press.

Levinson, B., Foley, D. E., & Holland, D. C. (Eds.). (1996). *The cultural production of the educated person: Critical ethnographies of schooling and local practice*. Albany: State University of New York Press.

Lindsey, R. (1985). The new Asian immigrants. In S. Anzovin (Ed.), *The problem of immigration* (pp. 13-27). New York: H. W. Wilson.

Losey, K. M. (1995). Mexican American students and classroom interaction: An overview and critique. *Review of Educational Research, 65,* 283-318.

Macias, J. (1990). Scholastic antecedents of immigrant students: Schooling in a Mexican immigrant-sending community. *Anthropology and Education Quarterly, 21,* 291-318.

Macias, J. (1996). Resurgence of ethnic nationalism in California and Germany: The impact on recent progress in education. *Anthropology and Education Quarterly, 27,* 232-252.

Margolis, M. L. (1994). *Little Brazil: An ethnography of Brazilian immigrants in New York City.* Princeton, NJ: Princeton University Press.

Martin, P., & Midgley, E. (1994). Immigration to the United States: Journey to an uncertain destination. *Population Bulletin, 49*(2), 2-46.

Martin, P., & Widgren, J. (1996). International migration: A global challenge. *Population Bulletin, 51*(1), 2-47.

Massey, D. S. (1993). Theories of international migration: A review and appraisal. *Population and Development Review, 19*(3), 431-466.

Matthijs, K. (1996). The socioeconomic assimilation of Caribbean American blacks. *Social Forces, 74*(3), 911-930.

Matute-Bianchi, M. E. (1986). Ethnic identities and patterns of success and failure among Mexican-descent and Japanese-American students in a California high school: An ethnographic analysis. *American Journal of Education, 95,* 233-255.

McCarthy, C., & Apple, M. W. (1988). Race, class, and gender in American educational research: Toward a nonsynchronous parallelist position. In L. Weis (Ed.), *Class, race, and gender in American education* (pp. 9-39). Albany: State University of New York Press.

McDermott, R. (1987). Achieving school failure: An anthropological approach to illiteracy and social stratification. In G. D. Spindler (Ed.), *Education and cultural process: Anthropological approaches* (pp. 173-209). Prospect Heights, IL: Waveland.

McDonnell, L. M., & Hill, P. T. (1993). *Newcomers in American Schools— Meeting the educational needs of immigrant youth.* Santa Monica, CA: RAND.

McNall, M., Dunnigan, T., & Mortimer, J. T. (1994). The educational achievement of the St. Paul Hmong. *Anthropology and Education Quarterly, 25*(1), 44-65.

Meisenheimer, J. R., II. (1992). How do immigrants fare in the U.S. labor market? *Monthly Labor Review, 115*(2), 3-19.

Melville, B. M. (1985). Salvadorans and Guatemalans. In D. W. Haines (Ed.), *Refugees in the United States: A reference handbook* (pp. 167-180). London: Greenwood.

Menchaca, M., & Valencia, R. R. (1990). Anglo-Saxon ideologies in the 1920s-1930s: Their impact on the segregation of Mexican students in California. *Anthropology and Education Quarterly, 21,* 222-249.

Model, S. (1991). Caribbean immigrants: A black success story? *International Migration Review, 24,* 248-276.

Montero-Sieburth, M., & LaCelle-Peterson, M. (1991). Immigration and schooling: An ethnohistorical account of policy and family perspectives in an urban community. *Anthropology and Education Quarterly, 22,* 300-325.

Morse, A. (1994). *America's newcomers.* Washington, DC: National Conference of State Legislatures.

Moscovici, S., & Paicheler, G. (1978). Social comparison and social recognition: Two complementary processes of identification. In H. Tajfel (Ed.), *Differentiation between social groups* (pp. 251-266). New York: Academic Press.

Neuman, K. E., & Tienda, M. (1994). The settlement and secondary migration patterns of legalized immigrants: Insights from administrative records. In B. Edmonston & J. S. Passel (Eds.), *Immigration and ethnicity: The adjustment of America's newest immigrants* (pp. 187-219). Washington, DC: Urban Institute.

Ogbu, J. U. (1978). *Minority education and caste: The American system in cross-cultural perspective.* New York: Academic Press.

Ogbu, J. U. (1982). Cultural discontinuities and schooling. *Anthropology and Education Quarterly, 13,* 290-307.

Ogbu, J. U. (1987). Variability in minority school performance: A problem in search of an explanation. *Anthropology and Education Quarterly, 18,* 312-334.

Ogbu, J. U. (1988). Class stratification, racial stratification, and schooling. In L. Weis (Ed.), *Class, race, and gender in American education* (pp. 163-182). Albany: State University of New York Press.

Ogbu, J. U., & Matute-Bianchi, M. E. (1986). Understanding sociocultural factors: Knowledge, identity, and school adjustment. In *Beyond language: Social and cultural factors in schooling language minority students* (pp. 73-142). Sacramento, CA: State Department of Education, Bilingual Education Office.

Paisano, E. (1993). *We the American Asians.* Washington, DC: U.S. Bureau of the Census.

Passel, J. S., & Edmonston, B. (1992). *Immigration and race in the United States: The 20th and 21st centuries.* Washington, DC: Urban Institute.

Passel, J. S., & Woodrow, K. (1984). Geographic distribution of undocumented immigrants: Estimates of undocumented aliens counted in the 1980 census by state. *International Migration Review, 18,* 642-671.

Pedraza, S. (1991). Women and migration: The social consequences of gender. *Annual Review of Sociology, 17,* 303-325.

Peng, S. S., & Wright, D. (1994). Explanation of academic achievement of Asian American students. *Journal of Educational Research, 87*(6), 346-352.

Perez, L. E. (1993). Opposition and the education of Chicana/os. In C. McCarthy & W. Crichlow (Eds.), *Race, identity, and representation in education* (pp. 268-279). New York: Routledge.

Peshkin, A. (1991). *The color of strangers, the color of friends: The play of ethnicity in school and community.* Chicago: University of Chicago Press.

Phelan, P., & Davidson, A. L. (Eds.). (1993). *Renegotiating cultural diversity in American schools.* New York: Teachers College Press.

Piore, M. J. (1979). *Birds of passage: Migrant labor and industrial societies.* New York: Cambridge University Press.

Portes, A., & Rumbaut, R. G. (1996). *Immigrant America: A portrait* (2nd ed.). Berkeley: University of California Press.

Portes, A., & Schauffler, R. (1994). Language and the second generation: Bilingualism yesterday and today. *International Migration Review, 28*(4), 640-661.

Portes, A., & Walton, J. (1981). *Labor, class, and the international system.* New York: Academic Press.

Portes, A., & Zhou, M. (1993, November). The new second generation: Segmented assimilation and its variants. *Annals of the American Academy of Political and Social Science, 530,* 74-96.

Ravitch, D. (1974). *The great school wars: A history of the New York City public schools.* New York: Basic Books.

Rodriguez, R. (1982). *Hunger of memory: The education of Richard Rodriguez.* New York: Bantam.

Rong, X. L. (1988). *Immigration and education in the United States, 1880-1980.* Unpublished doctoral dissertation, University of Georgia, Athens.

Rong, X. L. (1997, April). *Immigration, generation, gender, national origin, and schooling attainment among youths of six Asian American groups.* Paper presented at the annual meeting of the American Educational Research Association, Chicago, IL.

Rong, X. L., Brown, F., & Guo, X. (1996, April). *The effects of generation of U.S. residence on educational attainment among black and white youths.* Paper presented at the annual meeting of the American Educational Research Association, New York.

Rong, X. L., & Grant, L. (1992). Ethnicity, generation, and school attainment of Asians, Hispanics, and non-Hispanic whites. *Sociological Quarterly, 33*(4), 625-636.

Rong, X. L., & Grant, L. (1995, August). *Schooling attainment of Hispanic youth: Variations by national origin, generation of U.S. residence, and gender.* Paper presented at the annual meeting of the American Sociological Association, Washington, DC.

Rong, X. L., & Preissle, J. (1994, April). *Asian American teacher shortage: An overview and the solutions with the 1990 national data.* Paper presented at the annual meeting of the American Educational Research Association, New Orleans, LA.

Rong, X. L., & Preissle, J. (1997). The continuing decline in Asian American teachers. *American Educational Research Journal, 34*(2), 267-293.

Rumbaut, R. G. (1994). The crucible within: Ethnic identity, self-esteem, and segmented assimilation among children of immigrants. *International Migration Review, 28,* 748-794.

Silk, L. (1988, January 6). Economic scene. *New York Times,* p. 26.

Simon, J. (1984, February 27). Don't close our borders. *Newsweek,* p. 11.

Skerry, P. (1993). *Mexican Americans: The ambivalent minority.* Cambridge, MA: Harvard University Press.

Smith-Hefner, N. J. (1990). Language and identity in the education of Boston-area Khmer. *Anthropology and Education Quarterly, 21*(3), 250-268.

Smith-Hefner, N. J. (1993). Education, gender, and generational conflict among Khmer refugees. *Anthropology and Education Quarterly, 24*(2), 135-158.

Solomon, R. P. (1992). *Black resistance in high school: Forging a separatist culture.* Albany: State University of New York Press.

Spring, J. (1994). *American education.* New York: McGraw-Hill.

Stafford, S. B. (1987). Language and identity: Haitians in New York City. In C. R. Sutton & E. M. Chaney (Eds.), *Caribbean life in New York City: Sociocultural dimensions* (pp. 202-217). New York: Center for Migration Studies of New York.

Stepick, A., III, & Grenier, G. (1993). Cubans in Miami. In J. Moore & R. Pinderhughes (Eds.), *In the barrios: Latinos and the underclass debate* (pp. 79-100). New York: Russell Sage.

Stevens, G. (1992). The social and demographic contexts of language use in the U.S. *American Sociological Review, 57,* 171-185.

Stevens, G. (1994). The English language proficiency of immigrants in the U.S. In B. Edmonston & J. S. Passel (Eds.), *Immigration and ethnicity: The adjustment of America's newest immigrants* (pp. 163-185). Washington, DC: Urban Institute.

Stewart, D. W. (1993). *Immigration and education.* New York: Lexington.

Suarez-Orozco, C., & Suarez-Orozco, M. (1995). *Transformations: Migration, family life, and achievement motivation among Latino adolescents.* Stanford, CA: Stanford University Press.

Suarez-Orozco, M. M. (1987). Hispanic Americans: Comparative considerations and the educational problems of children. *International Migration Review, 25*(4), 141-163.

Suarez-Orozco, M. M. (1989). *Central American refugees and U.S. high schools: A psychosocial study of motivation and achievement.* Stanford, CA: Stanford University Press.

Sue, S., & Sue, D. W. (1973). Chinese-American personality and mental health. In S. Sue & N. N. Wagner (Eds.), *Asian Americans: Psychological perspectives* (pp. 111-124). Ben Lomand, CA: Science and Behavior Books.

Sung, L. B. (1987). *The adjustment experience of Chinese immigrant children in New York City.* New York: Center for Migration Studies.

Suzuki, B. (1977). Japanese-American experience. In M. J. Gold, C. A. Grant, & H. N. Rivlin (Eds.), *In praise of diversity: A resource book for multicultural education* (pp. 139-162). Washington, DC: Teacher Corps, Association of Teacher Educators.

Taeuber, I., & Taeuber, C. (1971). *People of the United States.* Washington, DC: U.S. Bureau of the Census.

Taft, R., & Cahill, D. (1981). Education of immigrants in Australia. In J. Bhatnagar (Ed.), *Educating immigrants* (pp. 16-46). New York: St. Martin's.

Thomas, B. (1954). *Migration and education growth.* Cambridge, UK: Cambridge University Press.

Thomas, B. (1968). Modern migration. In W. Adams (Ed.), *The brain drain* (pp. 29-49). New York: Macmillan.

Trueba, H. T. (1988). Culturally based explanations of minority students' academic achievement. *Anthropology and Education Quarterly, 19*, 270-287.

Trueba, H., Jacobs, L., & Kirton, E. (1990). *Cultural conflict and adaptation: The case of Hmong children in American society.* New York: Falmer.

U.S. Bureau of the Census. (1900). *Supplementary analysis.* Washington, DC: Government Printing Office.

U.S. Bureau of the Census. (1923). *Population, 1920, volume II: General report and analytical tables; Volume III: Composition and characteristics of the population by states.* Washington, DC: Government Printing Office.

U.S. Bureau of the Census. (1933). *Fifteenth census, U.S., 1930. Population report volume II, statistics by subjects.* Washington, DC: Government Printing Office.

U.S. Bureau of the Census. (1953). *Census of population: 1950. Volume II: Characteristics of the population, part 1, United States summary.* Washington, DC: Government Printing Office.

U.S. Bureau of the Census. (1963). *Census of population: 1960. Volume II: Characteristics of the population, part 1, United States summary.* Washington, DC: Government Printing Office.

U.S. Bureau of the Census. (1973). *Census of population: 1970, volume 1: Characteristics of the population, part 1, section 1-2; Detailed characteristics, pc (1)-D1.* Washington, DC: Government Printing Office.

U.S. Bureau of the Census. (1975). *Historical statistics of the United States. P. 118.* Washington, DC: Government Printing Office.

U.S. Bureau of the Census. (1981). *Current population survey: Public use tape file, November, 1979.* Washington, DC: Author.

U.S Bureau of the Census. (1983a). *Census of population: 1980. Volume 1, chapter B: General population characteristics, part 1, pc 80-1-B1; Chapter C: General social and economic characteristics, part 1, pc 80-1-C1; U.S. summary, pc 80-1-D1-A; Chapter D: Detailed population characteristics: Part 1, pc 80-1-D1.* Washington, DC: Government Printing Office.

U.S. Bureau of the Census. (1983b). *General social and economic characteristics, United States summary 1-63, Table 166.* Washington, DC: Author.

U.S. Bureau of the Census. (1985). *Statistical abstract of the United States, 1985.* Washington, DC: Author.

U.S. Bureau of the Census. (1993a). *U.S. summary: Population and housing summary, CPH-5-1; Social economic and housing characteristics, CPH-5-1 PT.1; General population characteristics; CP-1-1.* Washington, DC: Author.

U.S. Bureau of the Census. (1993b). *1990 census of population and housing—Public use microdata samples 5%.* Washington, DC: Author.

U.S. Bureau of the Census. (1996). *Statistical abstract of the United States, 1995.* Washington, DC: Government Printing Office.

U.S. Department of Education. (1984). *The condition of education, 1984.* Washington, DC: Author.

U.S. Department of Education. (1993a). *Digest of education statistics, 1993.* Washington, DC: Author.

U.S. Department of Education. (1993b). *The condition of education, 1993.* Washington, DC: Author.

Valentine, C. A. (1968). *Culture and poverty: Critique and counterproposals.* Chicago: University of Chicago Press.

Valverde, S. (1987). A comparative study of Hispanic high school dropouts and graduates: Why do some leave school early and some finish? *Education and Urban Society, 19,* 320-329.

Velez, W. (1989). High school attrition among Hispanic and non-Hispanic white youth. *Sociology of Education, 62*(2), 119-133.

Velez-Ibanez, C. G., & Greenberg, J. B. (1992). Formation and transformation of funds of knowledge among U.S.-Mexican households. *Anthropology and Education Quarterly, 23*(4), 313-335.

Verdonk, A. (1982). The children of immigrants in the Netherlands: Social position and implied risks for mental health. In R. Nann (Ed.), *Uprooting and surviving* (pp. 49-70). Boston: D. Reidel.

Villenas, S. (1996). The colonizer/colonized Chicana ethnographer: Identity, marginalization, and cooptation in the field. *Harvard Educational Review, 66*, 711-731.

Waggoner, D. (1991). *Undereducation in America.* New York: Auburn House.

Waters, M. C. (1991). The role of lineage in identity formation among black Americans. *Qualitative Sociology, 14*(1), 57-76.

Waters, M. C. (1994). Ethnic and racial identities of second-generation black immigrants in New York City. *International Migration Review, 28*, 795-820.

Wei, D. (1986). The Asian American success myth. *Interracial Books for Children, 17*(3 & 4), 16-17.

Wilson, W. J. (1987). *The truly disadvantaged.* Chicago: University of Chicago Press.

Woldemikael, T. M. (1989). *Becoming black American: Haitians and American institutions in Evanston, Illinois.* New York: AMS Press.

Zhou, M., & Bankston, C. L., III. (1994). Social capital and the adaptation of Vietnamese youth in New Orleans. *International Migration Review, 28*, 821-845.

Index

CORWIN
PRESS

The Corwin Press logo—a raven striding across an open book—
represents the happy union of courage and learning. We are a
professional-level publisher of books and journals for K–12 educators,
and we are committed to creating and providing resources that embody
these qualities. Corwin's motto is "Success for All Learners."

Please remember that this is a library book, and that it belongs only temporarily to each person who uses it. Be considerate. Do not write in this, or any, library book.

Date Due

OC 25 '00			
APR 2 8 2002			
OC 26 '0?			